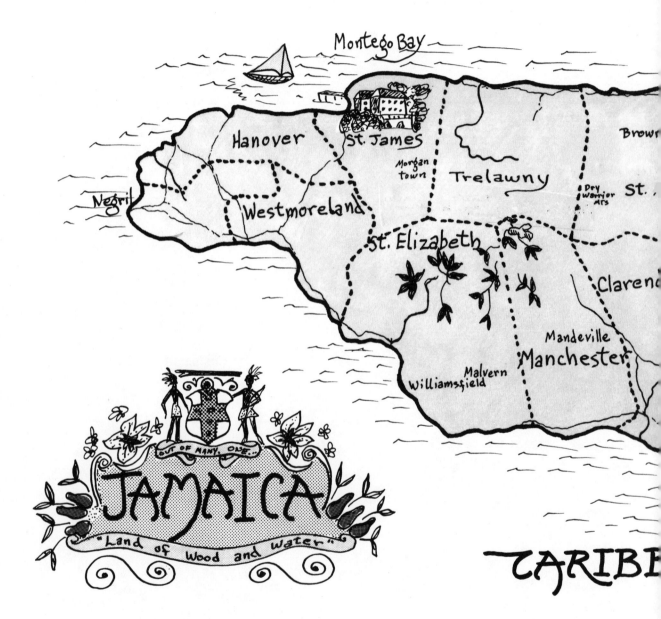

Montego Bay

Hanover

St. James

Browr

Morgan
town

Trelawny

Negri

Dry
Warrior
Mts

St. .

Westmoreland

St. Elizabeth

Clarend

Mandeville

Manchester

Williamsfield

Malvern

JAMAICA

"OUT OF MANY, ONE"

"Land of Wood and Water"

CARIBB

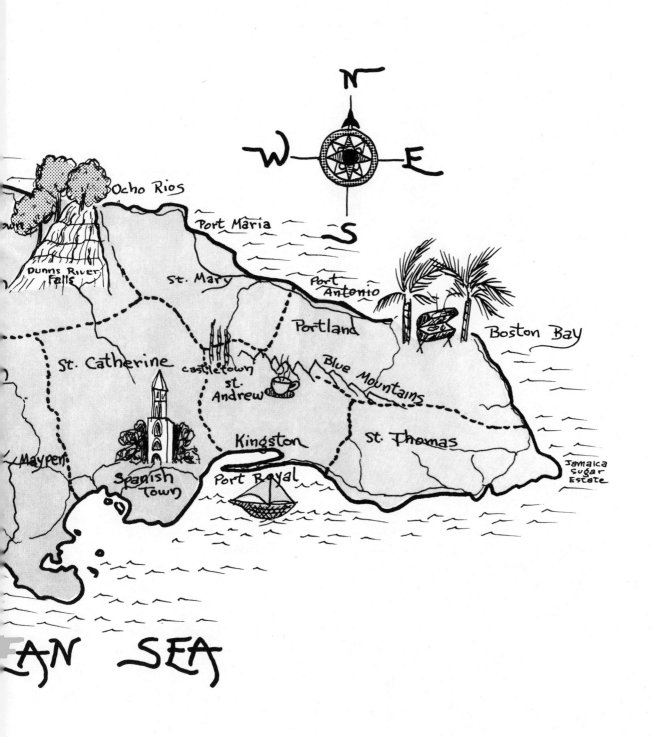

Jerk

Barbecue from Jamaica

Helen Willinsky

※ The Crossing Press • Freedom • California 95019

To my parents, George and Marion.

To my Aunt Monica, who began the typing of this manuscript in its embryonic stages on a very old, tiny, manual typewriter with a bubbling ribbon which we did not expect to last through even the first page.

To my husband, Hartmut, my children, Scott and Shana, my sister, Audrey, and my niece, Renee.

To my dear friends David and Eli at Sussex Estate, where my creativity for this whole jerk business came into being.

In appreciation to Mr. Deryck Cox, our New York Trade Commissioner; Mr. Max Silvera and Mr. Hans Schenk of the Half Moon Golf Club; Ms. Enid Donaldson, one of Jamaica's culinary experts; Mrs. Norma Benghiat, my school friend and expert on Jamaican cuisine; Ms. Monica Whyte, my darling aunt; and my dearly loved father, George Skinner. Special thanks to Mr. Dennis Hayes for his convincing idea and to Ms. Zou Feagin for her help and support. When you have so many wonderful, supportive friends, you can't fail!

Cover design by Nina Bookbinder
Cover photograph by Marti Griffin
Interior illustrations by Melanie Lofland Gendron

Printed in the U.S.A.

Library of Congress Cataloging-In-Publication Data

Willinsky, Helen.
    Jerk : barbecue from Jamaica / Helen Willinsky.
      p. cm.
    Includes index.
    ISBN 0-89594-440-5   ISBN 0-89594-439-1 (pbk.)
    1. Cookery, Jamaican. 2. Barbecue cookery. I. Title.
TX716.J27W55 1990
641.5'784'097292—dc20   90-40532
                         CIP

Contents

What is Jerk?

Jerk cooking is an authentic Jamaican way to cook pork, chicken, seafood, and beef over a fire pit or on a barbecue grill. But it is the special seasoning—a highly spiced combination of scallions, onions, thyme, Jamaican pimento (allspice), cinnamon, nutmeg, peppers, and salt—that makes jerk what it is. To me, jerk cooking is the perfect reflection of the Jamaican lifestyle—spicy, sweet, charismatic, and hot.

The taste of jerked foods is hot with peppers, but, as you savor it, the variety of spices catches up with you, and it is like a carnival where all the elements come together in your mouth. The combination of spices tastes as if they were quarreling and dancing and mingling in your mouth all at the same time. It is not a predictable flavor, but rather a hot, spicy, uncontrolled festival that engages all your senses. It is so unexpected a taste that, in spite of its peppery heat, you automatically want more. We have a saying in Jamaica, "It is very morish"—you want more.

People always ask me, "How did jerk get its name?" I really don't know, but I can tell you almost everyone has a pet theory. Some people say it is called jerk because the meat is turned over and over again—or jerked over and over again—as it cooks over the fire. Others say that is not right; it is called jerk because, when it is served, the jerk man pulls—or, you see, jerks—a portion of meat off the pork. To me, it does not matter what it is called, or why. What counts is flavor.

The spices that are used in jerk seasoning have a very special pungency. Jamaican spices are world famous—their oil content is said to be higher than anywhere else in the world, and it is the very oiliness of the spices that intensifies the zip and zest. (It is even said that in World War I, European soldiers were told to line their boots with Jamaican pimento as a way to make their feet warmer in the cold winters.)

Jerk huts are everywhere in Jamaica. You see them clustered by the side of the road, a medley of huts. There is always a wonderful smoky aroma hovering over the huts—the pungency of the burning pimento woods and spices mingling with the delicious scent of the meat. And everywhere are buses, trucks, cars, and vans disgorging hungry passengers in search of jerk pork, jerk chicken, escovitch fish, salt fish and ackee, roast yam, roast plantain, boiled corn, rice and peas, cock soup, mannish water, Irish moss, and festival! Everything that the Jamaicans love is found at the jerk huts, embellished with a great deal of spice. And the cries from each hut: "Which jerk you want?" "Taste mine!"

Jerk huts are usually octagonal or circular, with a telephone pole in the center supporting a thatched or shingled roof. There is a seating bar around the outside of the hut. The food is jerked outside, either in a lean-to attached to the hut, or in a separate hut of its own, or even under a tree. There is rarely any such thing as a parking lot—you park on the side of the road, and you are greeted warmly by the proprietor and the amiable strangers there. You will also see the other customers who are impatiently waiting to sink their teeth into the delicious slabs of meat.

All jerk huts and shacks are very casual affairs, but if it is an especially rustic jerk hut, you can saunter over and pick out what you want directly from the fire. The jerk man or lady will then use a cleaver to slice off whatever you have requested and probably will weigh it to know what to charge you. The meat is served wrapped in foil or on a paper plate. Pork is usually cubed for you on the spot and you stand right there and eat it with your fingers. Chicken tends to be a bit juicier than pork so you really need several napkins to handle that. Usually the meat is very tender because it has been marinated for some time and then cooked slowly. In addition to the pork and chicken, you can get some jerk sausage, and even jerked lobster if you are up on the northern coast of the island.

You must always eat jerk with something sweet or bland to cut the heat—either some festival, a little like a sweet hush puppy, or some hard dough bread, a soft, flat bagel-type bread. Of course, you must cool the mouth with Jamaican Red Stripe beer, Ting grapefruit soda, or a rum concoction. And there is usually music, music, music!

If you are in Jamaica, the best place to look for jerk is in Boston, near Boston Beach, the home of the original jerk pits. The Pork Pit in Montego Bay next to the Casa Montego Hotel (3½ miles from the Montego Bay Airport) and the Ocho Rios Jerk Center (6 Main Street, Ocho Rios) are also famous jerk pits. In Negril, jerk pits line the two main roads that lead in and out of town; in Port Antonio, look for jerk on West Street, near the market.

Jerking pork has been in Jamaica a long time, at least since the middle of the seventeenth century. The method of pit-cooking meat was brought to the island by African hunters who had been enslaved by the British. Quite possibly these West African hunters adapted the seasoning methods of the native Arawak Indians, especially in their use of chile peppers. But it was not until the middle of the eighteenth century, during the guerrilla wars between the escaped ex-slaves, known as Maroons, and England, that there was any real record of this method of preserving pork.

To the Maroon guerrilla bands, the little wild boars that darted through the bush were a wonderful source of food. While some men kept watch on movements of the Redcoats on the plains, others, equipped with long spears, undertook the equally arduous task of pursuing the slippery animals to their lairs in almost inaccessible parts of the mountains.

But caught and killed at last, the boars were brought down from the mountaintops on long sticks to provide food for the weary rebels. Although some meat was eaten at the time of the hunt, most had to be preserved until the next opportunity to hunt presented itself—and who could tell when that would be?

The jerk seasoning combination, laced heavily with salt and peppers, was a means of preservation. The pork was slathered with the aromatic spice combination and wrapped in leaves. Some buried the wrapped marinated pig in a hole in the ground filled with hot stones, and the pork would steam slowly in its own juices. Others would grill it slowly—oh, so slowly, for 12 or 14 hours—over a fire of green wood. This was jerk cooking.

A peace treaty was finally signed by the opposing forces, but jerking pork was now deep in the Jamaican psyche.

Nowadays, it is common to barbecue pork over pimento wood to give the flesh that tangy flavor inherent in the pimento tree; but it was not always so. Those early Maroons used not only the wood of another tree, but also a number of strange herbs to season the meat. The practice was always secret and, even today, if one asked the descendant of a Maroon where his wood and those herbs could be found, he would wave his hand vaguely to the surrounding hills, and say, "Over there."

This wonderful secret way to prepare meat became part of the Jamaican life-style only about 15 years ago. Now there are jerk huts everywhere—in every town, every village, in every city in Jamaica.

Jerking is the latest food craze sweeping the island. It is no longer confined to pork, but now includes fish and chicken. Although jerk pork originally led the field, jerk chicken is now most popular. In Kingston, the capital of Jamaica, the demand for jerk chicken on the weekends is incredible. The steel drums converted to grills are now ubiquitous. They line the streets and, on a weekend in certain sections of Red Hills Road, so much smoke emerges from the line of drums that, except for the smell, one could be forgiven for thinking that a San Francisco fog had come to Jamaica.

To eat jerk is to feel the influences from which it developed. It is as if you can hear the African, Indian, and calypso cultures that produced it. Jamaicans are great harmonizers—we make delicious soups, we keep our friends forever, we are fantastic musicians and artists—and we have applied this same harmony to our jerk seasoning.

All Jamaicans have their own variations on the jerk theme. "Come and taste my jerk chicken," we hear again and again. "It is better than the last time I saw you." Some make mixes that are liquid marinades, others are thick pastes, and some are rubs to be massaged into the meats. But all these concoctions can be made at home so that you can come up with your own version of jerk cooking. So you see, you don't have to go to a Jamaican jerk hut to enjoy jerk. You can make it, as we in Jamaica do, in your own kitchen.

Jerking Basics & Jerk Seasonings

In this chapter, I will give you recipes for seasoning and marinating your foods in the flavor of Jamaican jerk, and I will give you some cooking pointers. With the jerk seasonings, you can make authentic-tasting jerk in your backyard barbecue, or in your oven, or in a stove-top smoker.

It is simple. I will show you how.

If you want to go to Jamaica to see how jerk is made, you will have to visit a jerk pit. You see, a pit is dug and in it a fire is made mainly with the wood of the pimento (allspice) tree. The meat is slathered with seasonings and left to marinate. When the fire is ready, the meat is wrapped in foil, then covered with the burning coals. This process allows the meat to cook more by smoke than by heat. The meat cooks for several hours until it is tender. This was the way the original jerk pork was done and is still being done today.

Then there are the jerk huts, which have mushroomed throughout the entire island. They serve all the varying jerk dishes, which they prepare on an open barbecue grill over extremely hot coals; really they make an island barbecue. Marinated chicken or whole fish will cook slowly for 30 to 40 minutes. Pork roasts, flattened, and covered with spices, will slowly smoke as they are grilled for 2 to 3 hours.

Types of Grills

Some vendors use old oil drums for jerking. They cover the drum with pieces of zinc roofing so that the juices and smoke keep the chicken or pork tender. At the end of the cooking time, the cover is removed, and the meat grills to a crisp finish. This is my favorite method, because the pork or chicken is tender on the inside and crisp on the outside.

You can recreate a similar product in your home by roasting the meat in a very slow oven (275° F.) for 1 to 2 hours, and then finishing it off on the outdoor grill. The baking process can also be done in the microwave and finished off on the grill.

Grill Cooking

In Jamaica, 50-gallon drums are converted into grills. The chicken prepared on it is known as "pan chicken." The same flavor can be achieved on a backyard barbecue grill. Use charcoal, wood, or gas, and place the food 3 to 5 inches above the fire, depending on how fast the food needs to cook.

If you are using charcoal, don't fill the grill with more fuel than you need, as is common for most people. It takes longer to light and burn down, and then the fire lasts long after you are finished cooking. Spread out enough charcoal in one layer so there will be heat under all the food, then pile up the charcoal to do the actual lighting. When you are ready to cook, about 30 minutes after you have lit the fire, spread out the coals again.

For smoking, or slow cooking, place a drip pan in the center of the grill and arrange the coals around the drip pan. The food will go on the grill directly over the drip pan. (This is also a good way to prevent flare-ups when cooking high-fat foods.) The juices that drip into the pan can be collected and poured over the meat for additional flavor and moistness. For an even cooler fire, put the charcoal next to, not around, the drip pan, and place the meat over the drip pan. With a dual-control gas grill, turn on one side and cook on the other.

Adding wood chips to your fire will provide additional flavor. Just soak a generous handful of chips in water first so they don't burn up immediately. Throw them over the coals any time during cooking and cover the grill, if possible, for 5 to 10 minutes so that the smoke permeates the meat. If pimento (allspice) wood from the Islands is not available, try apple wood, mesquite, or the familiar hickory chip, which is still the most available and least expensive. Wood chip smoking will enhance all of the dishes.

We generally cover our grills with a sheet of zinc roofing to capture the smoke and keep the meat from drying out. You can fashion a loose tent of aluminum foil to achieve the same effect.

Open Pit Cooking

If you really want to recreate the true Jamaican jerk, you must get out your shovel and get to work. Dig a pit that is about 2 feet deep. A few hours before you are ready to eat, build a wood fire in the pit. In Jamaica we use pimento (allspice) wood, or a combination of pimento wood and charcoal, but you can use any type of hardwood. Wait until the wood has burned down to coals and you have a low smoky fire before you begin to cook. From time to time, you will want to add more wood to the fire, but keep the fresh burning wood away from the cooking meat—the heat should be indirect.

Place the cooking grid approximately $1^1/_2$ feet over the fire and put the meat on. A pork roast will take about 2 hours to cook, a whole chicken will take about an hour, and whole fish will cook in 20 to 30 minutes, depending on its size. As the meat cooks, jerk it, or turn it frequently.

Stove-Top Smokers

Not everyone can live in Jamaica, where the weather is suitable for outdoor grilling year-round. If this applies to you, perhaps you would be interested in acquiring a stove-top smoker. With your meat seasoned with jerk spices, a stove-top smoker will bring you closest to jerk pit flavors.

A stove-top smoker, or water pan smoker, consists of a stack of pans. The bottom pan holds soaked wood chips. Above that is a pan that holds water, vinegar, wine, or fruit juice—whatever you want to use to flavor your meat. In the top pan is a grid on which you place the meat. The water (or other cooking liquid) combines with the charcoal smoke to make a smoky fog that infuses the meat with great flavor. To use, follow the manufacturer's directions. Generally, it takes about 20 minutes to cook 4 chicken breasts on a stove-top smoker. It takes 10 to 20 minutes to cook a batch of shrimp.

Meat prepared with a water smoker will be moist and tender. I like to finish the meat on a grill or under a broiler to get a crisp coating, but that is not necessary.

Controlling the Heat

I think meat is most delicious when it is cooked slowly over a fire that is not very hot. A very hot fire will char the meat on the outside and leave it raw on the inside. You can control the heat by adjusting the height of the grill above the fire and by allowing the fire to burn down to coals before you start cooking. My Aunt Becky taught me that when the fire is just the right temperature you can hold your hand just above the grill (about 1 inch above the grill) for 3 to 6 seconds before you start to burn. A slow fire, which is required for thicker pieces of meat and whole pieces of chicken, will allow you to hold your hand over the fire for about 4 to 8 seconds.

Sometimes when the oil from the marinade or the fat from the meat itself drips onto the hot coals, a flame will flare up and char the meat. You can control flare-ups by sprinkling with water from a spray bottle kept handy for that purpose. A drip pan to catch the fat as it drips off will also prevent flare-ups.

How to Tell When Your Jerk is Done

When barbecuing or grilling any meat, the most difficult thing to gauge is when the food is done. Timings can be given in recipes, but whether the meat is at room temperature or refrigerator-cold when placed on the grill, how thick the meat or fish is cut, how hot the fire burns, and how far from the fire the grill is laid will all affect timing. Even the weather affects timing.

Experienced cooks can judge how done meat is by feel. Well-done meat will feel as firm as the flesh on the palm of your hand. Fish should be white and firm to the touch. Juices from poultry should run clear, not red, when the flesh is pricked with a fork. Only experience will enable you to judge when to remove meat, chicken, and fish from a grill.

An instant-read thermometer (available in most kitchen supply stores) is a big help in determining when roasts and whole birds are done.

Jerk Flavors

After years of studying culinary arts in Europe, I returned to Jamaica in 1969 to begin work as a hotel manager with my husband, Hartmut. We were asked to manage a wonderful resort called Goblin Hill in Portland. It was an idyllic setting and we developed a reputation for having the finest food on that side of the Island.

On our way to work each day we would pass by a jerk stand—primitive, oh, so primitive—in Boston. Now you must remember that back then jerk cooking had none of the popularity it enjoys today.

One day when I saw the jerk stand, I said, "Willinsky, let us recreate this whole feeling at the hotel—the jerk pork, the beer, the music, the people." So we instituted Sunday afternoon parties where we served rum punch and Boston jerk to hotel guests.

Charles and Tony, our jerk pork experts, would prepare the seasoning the night before, using Aunt Becky's finger-licking recipe. She has the most wonderful jerk spice combination, which she would pound in a mortar and slather over her pork and chicken.

On Sunday, the meat would be grilled in a billowing cloud of aromatic smoke. A piece of zine roofing would loosely cover the grill, which would capture the smoke and help to keep the meat moist. It is the smoke that captivates. The smell is created by the secret recipe and the smoke from the pimento wood. Now I will share with you the secret recipes.

Jerk Rub

1 onion, finely chopped
½ cup finely chopped
   scallion
2 teaspoons fresh thyme
   leaves
2 teaspoons salt
1 teaspoon ground
   Jamaican pimento
   (allspice)
¼ teaspoon ground nutmeg
½ teaspoon ground
   cinnamon
4 to 6 hot peppers, finely
   ground
1 teaspoon ground black
   pepper

Pastes made of spices, herbs, and onions are the authentic jerk flavoring method. You rub the paste into the uncooked meat to add flavor. This is a medium-hot paste; it can be made hotter with the addition of more hot peppers or hot pepper sauce. If you want less heat, remove the seeds and membranes containing the seeds from the peppers before grinding them. Scotch bonnet or habañero peppers are preferred, but you can substitute the milder, more readily available jalapeño or serrano peppers.

Mix together all the ingredients to make a paste. A food processor fitted with a steel blade is ideal for this. Store leftovers in the refrigerator in a tightly closed jar for about a month.

YIELD: ABOUT 1 CUP

Jerk Marinade

1 onion, finely chopped
½ cup finely chopped
    scallion
2 teaspoons fresh thyme
    leaves
1 teaspoon salt
2 teaspoons sugar
1 teaspoon ground
    Jamaican pimento
    (allspice)
½ teaspoon ground nutmeg
½ teaspoon ground
    cinnamon
1 hot pepper, finely
    ground
1 teaspoon ground black
    pepper
3 tablespoons soy sauce
1 tablespoon cooking oil
1 tablespoon cider or
    white vinegar

Some people find marinades more convenient to use than spice pastes. This marinade is more liquid than a paste, but not as liquid as most marinades. The flavor of the marinade may strike you as a little harsh when you first mix it, but I assure you, the flavors will all blend and mellow as the meat cooks. To increase the heat of this rather mild marinade, add hot pepper sauce. If you want less heat, remove the seeds and membranes containing the seeds from the peppers before grinding them.

Mix together all the ingredients. A food processor fitted with a steel blade is ideal for chopping and combining. This will provide an excellent marinade for chicken, beef, or pork. Store leftover marinade in the refrigerator in a tightly closed jar for about 1 month.

YIELD: ABOUT 1½ CUPS

15

Dry Jerk Seasoning

1 tablespoon onion flakes
1 tablespoon onion powder
2 teaspoons ground thyme
2 teaspoons salt
1 teaspoon ground
  pimento (allspice)
¼ teaspoon ground nutmeg
¼ teaspoon ground
  cinnamon
2 teaspoons sugar
1 teaspoon coarsely
  ground black pepper
1 teaspoon cayenne pepper
2 teaspoons dried chives or
  green onions

This seasoning mix is excellent to have on hand to sprinkle on cooked or uncooked fish, vegetables, or snacks. It does not have quite as strong a flavor as the rub and the marinade. To increase the heat, add more cayenne.

Mix together all the ingredients. Store leftovers in a tightly closed glass jar. It will keep its pungency for over a month.

YIELD: 5 TABLESPOONS

Jamaican Ingredients

Most of the ingredients used in this cookbook are easily found in supermarkets across the country. Some are more likely to be found in stores that cater to a Hispanic clientele, and a few may need to be special ordered. You will find a listing of sources of Jamaican ingredients in the back of this book. Let me explain about some of the more unusual ingredients. Breadfruit, callaloo, plantains, sweet potatoes, and yams are all served as side dishes with jerk. These are explained in detail in chapter 6, "Wid It."

Pimento, or Allspice

Many cooks in America think that allspice is a blend of cinnamon, nutmeg, and cloves because that is the aroma given off by the berries. But, in fact, allspice is the fruit of the pimento tree, which grows wild in the Caribbean. When Spanish explorers came across the berries, they named the spice pimento, because the dried allspice berries look like large peppercorns. Botanists named the tree *Pimenta officinalis*. So in Jamaica, what we call pimento, you call allspice; and the spice is readily available in any supermarket, whole or ground.

Allspice, or Jamaican pimento, is one of the key ingredients in jerk flavorings. If you want true Jamaican flavor, then you must seek out a source for imported Jamaican pimento. Jamaican pimento is more pungent than the same berry grown elsewhere. The oil content is much higher and that gives the spice its special flavor. There are supermarket spice brands that specify Jamaican allspice.

Coconut

In Jamaica, nobody bothers with packages of dried coconut such as you see in the baking department of most U.S. supermarkets. We use fresh coconuts, and they are quite easy to prepare. Here are some helpful tips.

To make grated fresh coconut, take a large coconut without any cracks and containing liquid (shake it to hear the water sloshing). Pierce the eyes of the coconut with an ice pick or a skewer. Drain the liquid and reserve it for another use (especially Rum and Coconut Water, page 155).

Bake the coconut in a preheated 400° F. oven for 15 minutes. This will cause the flesh to shrink from the shell and make it easy to remove. Break the coconut with a hammer and remove the flesh from the shell, flipping it out carefully with a strong knife. Peel off the brown membrane with a vegetable peeler. Then cut the coconut meat into small pieces. In a blender or food processor fitted with a steel blade, grind the pieces, a few at a time. (Or grate the meat on the fine side of a grater.) You should have about 4 cups.

To make thick fresh coconut milk, put 2 cups of cubed fresh coconut in a blender or food processor fitted with a steel blade and process. Add 1¼ cups very hot water and blend for 1 minute in the blender or for 2 minutes in the food processor. Let the mixture cool for at least 5 minutes. Strain it through a fine sieve lined with a double thickness of rinsed and squeezed cheesecloth, pressing hard on the solids to extract as much liquid as you can. Bring the corners of the cheesecloth together and squeeze the remaining milk through the sieve into the bowl. Makes about 1½ cups. In a pinch, you can make coconut milk from packaged sweetened flaked coconut. This yields a sweet milk that would be suitable for desserts but not for savory dishes.

Making fresh coconut milk is time-consuming. If you can find unsweetened canned or frozen coconut milk in a local store or through the mail order sources in the back of this book, you can use that to save time. Stores that cater to Asians, particularly Thais, and Hispanics are most likely to carry coconut milk.

Some of the recipes call for cream of coconut. This is a sweetened coconut milk available canned in most supermarkets. Look for the Goya or Coco Lopez label. Sometimes cream of coconut is called piña colada mix. Do not substitute cream of coconut for coconut milk.

Hot Peppers

We Jamaicans like our foods spicy hot. The heat comes from hot peppers, *Capsicum sinensis*. We use Scotch bonnets and bird peppers—a bad, bad pepper. The medium-sized Scotch bonnet is a flavorful thick-skinned round pepper; it may be red, yellow, or green. There is an almost identical pepper called the habañero, which is raised in Mexico and the Yucatan and can be found in many Spanish markets. These peppers are the best substitutes for Scotch bonnets. You can substitute jalapeño peppers if you must. Many recipes call for adding the hot pepper whole and removing it after the dish is cooked. In this way, we get the flavor of the pepper without the heat. If you want less heat, in recipes calling for sliced or ground pepper, remove the seeds and the membranes containing the seeds from the pepper.

A fresh hot pepper and a sharp knife are always served on the side of the plate so that diners can sliver off pieces of pepper as their palate allows.

Hot pepper sauces can always be used to spice up dishes.

Scotch bonnet pepper sauce is preferred for most dishes and to add heat to the basic Jerk Marinade (page 15) and Jerk Rub (page 14). (Sources for Scotch bonnet pepper sauce are listed in the back of this book.) Pickapeppa Sauce is another Jamaican pepper sauce that can add heat to your food. If your grocer doesn't carry it, you can write the U.S. distributor (Warbac Sales Company, PO Box 9279, Metairie, LA 70055) for the location of someone near you who does.

Tamarind

The 30-foot-tall tamarind tree yields a seedpod that contains a flavorful, acidic pulp which is used to flavor drinks and condiments. It is one of the key ingredients in Worcestershire sauce.

Tamarind can be bought fresh in Hispanic and Asian markets. Middle Eastern food stores often carry the pulp in plastic-wrapped blocks. You can also find the drink in cans in the supermarket under the Goya label.

Ginger

We use fresh Jamaican ginger root in many recipes. This is not quite the same ginger root called for in many Chinese recipes. Jamaican ginger root is very pungent and robust; Chinese ginger root is lighter and fresher in flavor. Substitute Chinese ginger root if Jamaican ginger root is unavailable.

Because ginger is so irregularly shaped, it is sometimes hard to measure it exactly. That's okay; exact measurements aren't important. In Jamaica, we usually measure ginger in terms of the hand. A knuckle of ginger is approximately the length of the knuckle of your finger: 3/4 to 1 inch. A finger, as you can guess, is approximately 3 inches long. A full hand of ginger is a bony-shaped piece that is usually 4 to 6 inches long and may have some "fingers" coming off it.

Chocho

If you can't find chochos at your local produce store, try asking for chayote, or christophene, or mirliton. One of those names might be the one under which this bland, pear-shaped squash is found. Botanists call the chocho a "one-seeded cucumber" and sometimes you can substitute cucumber for chocho.

If you have the choice, select the female chocho, which has a smooth, tender skin; the male chocho has a furrowed, prickly skin. Chocho is added to soups and stews, and can be pureed, stuffed, baked, creamed, or steamed.

Pork Tails & Tales

Butterflied Pork Loin on the Grill

Jamaican Jerk Barbecued Ribs

Glazed Spareribs

Jerked Oriental Spareribs

Pork-Pineapple Kabobs

Roasted Pork

Roasted Pork Tenderloin

Oriental-Style Roast Pork

Jerked Roasted Suckling Pig

Medallions of Pork

Jerked Pork Chops & Fruited Rice Pilaf

Pork & Mango Curry

Smoked Fresh Ham

Long before pigs in Jamaica were domesticated, Christopher Columbus discovered Arawaks cooking small wild boars over hot coals buried in the ground. Later, the special barbecuing of the pig was confined to Maroon Town, a village on the 7,800-foot-high Blue Mountain in the parish of Portland, the home of the former slaves. But over time the Maroons lost their monopoly on barbecuing pork because jerking had become extremely popular. Others took up the method and gradually the practice of jerking found its way down the mountainside until it reached Boston Beach in Port Antonio. This beach is a well-known bathing strip a few miles out of Port Antonio, the capital of Portland. It is heavily frequented by people from Kingston, 70 miles away, as well as by a considerable number of tourists.

Undoubtedly, the best jerk on the island is made by the man who has a pit by the side of the road there. It is a corrugated zinc shed, open on all sides, in which 2 pigs are being constantly barbecued, from midmorning to night. The smell, the heat, the pungency, is marvelous. Devotees, most of them in bathing suits, never leave. No matter how long it takes, they wait until the master says "A' ready now" and begins to cut. "How much yo' want? Quarter pound, half pound?" and his long knife begins to slice through the tender meat.

They are devotees, indeed. So hot is the meat, reeking with black pepper, and Scotch bonnet pepper, that it can hardly be eaten. The smallest taste is enough to make the eyes water. The palate can tolerate the fiery substance only after repeated attempts.

Boston Beach jerk pork is the most authentic jerk in Jamaica. There are other pits—in Ocho Rios, 60 miles away, in Montego Bay, a further 60, and in Negril, still a further 60, but it is acknowledged that they cannot rival the jerk of Boston Beach.

But if you cannot come to Boston Beach, at least you can jerk pork in your own backyard!

Butterflied Pork Loin on the Grill

4-pound boneless pork loin roast

2 onions, finely chopped

1 tablespoon fresh thyme leaves

½ teaspoon ground Jamaican pimento (allspice)

¼ teaspoon ground nutmeg

¼ teaspoon ground cinnamon

1 tablespoon sugar

2 tablespoons hot pepper sauce

¼ cup soy sauce

2 tablespoons oil

Crisp on the outside, tender and moist inside. This easy-to-prepare pork loin is perfect for parties.

Trim any excess fat from the pork roast. Butterfly the roast by cutting horizontally through the center. Or, if in doubt, ask your butcher to butterfly it for you. The meat should lie flat. Place the pork in a flat dish.

Combine the remaining ingredients to make a jerk paste. Spread the paste over the pork loin, cover, and marinate in the refrigerator for at least 4 hours.

Prepare a fire in the grill. When the coals have burned down and are medium hot, place the pork on the grill with foil under it to catch the drippings. The roast should cook over medium coals for approximately 2 hours or until a meat thermometer reads 150° to 160° F.

Cut the butterflied pork loin in half lengthwise. Carve into thin slices. Serve with roasted sweet potatoes and Jamaican Cole Slaw (page 115). Don't forget to roast your sweet potatoes in the coals with the meat!

YIELD: 8 TO 10 SERVINGS

Jamaican Jerk Barbecued Ribs

1 cup Jerk Marinade
(page 15)
1 tablespoon sugar
2 tablespoons red wine
vinegar
4 pounds pork spareribs
About 1½ cups barbecue
sauce

In this recipe, I combine the jerk flavors with barbecue sauce. The sauce, added during the final 15 minutes of cooking adds a delicious crust to the succulent ribs. Any store-bought barbecue sauce will do, or you can use the barbecue sauce I use on chickens (see page 47).

Combine the Jerk Marinade, sugar, and vinegar. Add the ribs and turn to coat thoroughly. Marinate in the refrigerator for at least 4 hours.

Prepare a fire in the grill. When the coals have burned down, rake the coals to the sides. Set a drip pan in the center of the grill and arrange the coals around it to provide indirect heat. Place the ribs on the grill over the drip pan, and cook for 1½ hours, turning and brushing frequently with the marinade. Brush the ribs with the commercial barbecue sauce during the last 15 minutes of cooking.

Serve with Rice and Peas (page 112) and a salad. Add lots of brightly colored napkins, Jamaican Red Stripe beer, and reggae music.

YIELD: 4 SERVINGS

Glazed Spareribs

About 6 pounds pork
   spareribs
1½ cups Jerk Marinade
   (page 15)
2 cups apple jelly
1 cup water
1 teaspoon curry powder

In the Jamaican melting pot are many people who are of East Indian descent. From them we have learned to make all kinds of delicious curries and to use curry powder to good effect. The two-part cooking process makes these ribs especially tender and great for parties when you don't want to spend all your time at the grill.

Combine the spareribs with the Jerk Marinade and marinate in the refrigerator for 2 to 3 hours. (Or for a less pungent flavor, pour the marinade over ribs just before cooking.)

Preheat the oven to 350° F. Arrange the marinated spareribs meaty side down on a baking sheet. Bake for 1 hour, turning once if needed. This part of the preparation can be done the day before.

Prepare a fire in the grill. Prepare the glaze by combining the apple jelly, water, and curry powder in a small saucepan. Bring to a boil. Cook slowly for about 3 minutes. Remove from the heat and keep warm.

Put the ribs on the grill, meaty side up. Spread the glaze lightly over the ribs. Cook for 5 to 10 minutes, or until the bottom is crisp. Turn and glaze lightly again. Continue cooking until nicely browned. Coat again with the glaze after taking from the grill. Serve hot.

YIELD: 6 SERVINGS

Jerked Oriental Spareribs

4 pounds pork spareribs
2 teaspoons salt
2 tablespoons sugar
⅓ cup rice wine or dry
  sherry
⅓ cup soy sauce
3 tablespoons Jerk Rub
  (page 14)

Oriental foods are very popular in Jamaica. This delicious recipe for spareribs uses rice wine and soy sauce. You can bake these ribs in the oven or grill them on a barbecue grill.

Cut the pork into individual ribs. In a shallow ovenproof dish, combine the ribs with the remaining ingredients. Cover and let stand in the refrigerator for 1 hour, turning once or twice.

Preheat the oven to 400° F. or prepare a fire in the grill.

Bake the ribs for 40 to 45 minutes, or until tender, turning and basting once. Or barbecue the ribs on a grill over white hot coals for 20 to 25 minutes, basting and turning every 10 minutes or so, until browned. With a cleaver, chop each rib into 2 or 3 small pieces. Serve hot.

YIELD: 4 SERVINGS

Pork-Pineapple Kabobs

1½-pound boneless pork
  loin, cubed
¾ cup Jerk Marinade
  (page 15)
1 fresh pineapple, peeled,
  cored, and cut into
  cubes
2 green bell peppers,
  cubed
12 little pearl onions

The fresh fruit adds a wonderful, sweet flavor to the kabobs.

Combine the pork and Jerk Marinade in a resealable plastic bag. Rotate the bag several times to coat the meat with the marinade. Marinate for several hours in the refrigerator.

Prepare a fire in the grill. While you are waiting for the grill to heat, add the pineapple and vegetables to the meat and marinade. If you are using bamboo skewers, soak for 20 to 30 minutes to prevent charring while cooking.

Skewer the pork and vegetables alternately on metal or bamboo skewers. Cook over white hot coals for approximately 5 minutes on each side, basting occasionally. Serve hot.

YIELD: 4 SERVINGS

Roasted Pork

2 garlic cloves, finely
   chopped
¼ cup soy sauce
1 hot pepper, chopped, or
   1 tablespoon hot pepper
   sauce
½ teaspoon dried thyme
½ teaspoon ground
   Jamaican pimento
   (allspice)
1 boneless pork loin roast
   (3 to 4 pounds)

This pork is roasted in the oven, but the flavor is typical of jerk cooking. I like to serve this with the Honey-Ginger Dipping Sauce (page 118). Roast the meat for 20 to 25 minutes per pound, or until the internal temperature reaches 150° to 160° F.

Mix together the garlic, soy sauce, hot pepper, thyme, and pimento. Smear seasoning on the pork. In Jamaica, we also pierce the pork, putting some of the seasoning inside the meat so that the flavor will penetrate. Cover and refrigerate overnight to allow the meat to marinate.

When you are ready to roast, preheat the oven to 350° F. Place the meat in a roasting pan and loosely cover with foil. Roast for 1 hour, and then uncover and continue roasting for 30 to 45 minutes more, or until the internal temperature reaches 150° to 160° F. Transfer the pork to a platter and let it stand for 10 minutes before carving.

YIELD: 8 TO 10 SERVINGS

Roasted Pork Tenderloin

2 tablespoons finely
   chopped scallion greens
1 teaspoon fresh thyme
   leaves
1 teaspoon salt
¼ teaspoon ground
   Jamaican pimento
   (allspice)
Pinch ground nutmeg
Pinch ground cinnamon
2 teaspoons hot pepper
   sauce
1 tablespoon soy sauce
1 teaspoon sugar
1½-pound pork
   tenderloin, trimmed

Another oven roast for those who can't barbecue year-round. I like to serve this with the Tamarind-Apricot Sauce (page 120) to which I add a dollop of Dijon-style mustard. Pork tenderloins are quick cooking and very tender.

Preheat the oven to 350° F.

Mix all the ingredients, except the pork, to make a jerk paste. Place the tenderloin in a flat baking dish, and smear the jerk paste over it. Roast immediately for 30 to 45 minutes, or until a meat thermometer registers 150° to 160° F. The meat will be cooked through but still juicy. Slice the meat against the grain and serve with baked potatoes and tossed salad.

YIELD: 4 SERVINGS

Oriental-Style Roast Pork

2 tablespoons soy sauce
1 teaspoon light or dark
   rum
2 tablespoons catsup
2 teaspoons Jerk Rub
   (page 14)
3 tablespoons chicken
   stock or broth
1 tablespoon sugar
1½-pound pork
   tenderloin, trimmed
1¼ cups Honey-Ginger
   Dipping Sauce (page
   118)

In a small, deep dish just large enough to hold the pork, combine the soy sauce, rum, catsup, Jerk Rub, chicken stock, and sugar. Mix thoroughly. Add the pork, turning it to completely cover with the marinade. Cover and marinate in the refrigerator for about 3 hours. Bring to room temperature before roasting.

Preheat the oven to 350° F.

Arrange the pork in a roasting pan and roast for 35 minutes. Meanwhile, prepare the Honey-Ginger Dipping Sauce. Pour some of it over the pork roast and roast for an additional 10 minutes, or until a meat thermometer reaches 150° to 160° F. Transfer the meat to a cutting board and let it stand for 10 minutes. Carve the pork against the grain into thin slices and arrange on a heated platter. Serve with plain boiled rice and pass the remaining Honey-Ginger Dipping Sauce on the side.

YIELD: 4 SERVINGS

Jerked Roasted Suckling Pig

Jerk Paste

4 onions, finely chopped
2 cups finely chopped
   scallions
4 tablespoons dried thyme
   leaves
¼ cup salt
2 tablespoons ground Jamaican pimento (allspice)
½ teaspoon ground nutmeg
1 teaspoon ground cinnamon
4 hot peppers, seeded
1 tablespoon ground black
   pepper
½ cup vegetable oil
6 garlic cloves

Pig

1 suckling pig, dressed and
   well cleaned (approxi-
   mately 10 pounds)
Vegetable oil
Salt
Pepper

Stuffing

2 or 3 white potatoes, cooked
   and mashed
2 or 3 sweet potatoes, cooked
   and mashed
2 or 3 tablespoons butter

Roasted suckling pig is one of the dishes that is served when we entertain lavishly for large gatherings at weddings, hotel buffets, Christmas parties, and New Year's Eve parties. Generally, it is prepared and brought in by someone who specializes in "roast pig." Traditionally, a suckling pig is roasted on a spit over a wood fire, but if you have a large enough oven, you can prepare a suckling pig at home.

Preheat the oven to 350° F.

Combine the paste ingredients in a food processor to make a paste. Rub the inside of the pig with the paste, reserving approximately 1 tablespoon to mix with the stuffing. Rub the outside of the pig with oil, salt, and pepper.

Mix together the white, sweet potatoes, butter, and remaining 1 tablespoon jerk paste until well blended. Loosely pack the stuffing inside the pig and close the opening with skewers or sew together. Draw the legs back and tie with string. Stuff the mouth with a piece of aluminum foil to keep it open as it roasts.

Place the pig on a rack in a large baking pan, so that the fat will drain off and the skin will remain crisp. Roast until done, allowing 15 minutes per pound, or for 2 to 2½ hours. The internal temperature should reach 165° F., and the juices should run clear if you pierce the thigh with a fork or the tip of a small knife.

Remove the pig from the oven and place on a heated platter. Remove the foil from the mouth and replace it with an apple.

Let the pig rest at room temperature for 10 to 15 minutes before carving.

Serve this roasted pig with baked plantains and roasted breadfruit.

YIELD: 12 TO 15 SERVINGS

Medallions of Pork

1 tablespoon Dry Jerk
   Seasoning (page 16)
2 pounds boneless pork
   loin chops
2 tablespoons vegetable oil
2 large firm apples, cored
   and sliced ½ inch thick
Tamarind-Apricot Sauce
   (page 120, prepared
   with the optional
   mustard)

These pork medallions are fast cooking and relatively inexpensive to make since there is no bone or other waste. You can make this a complete meal by adding sweet potato slices in with the pork and apples. This is wonderful with Jamaican Cole Slaw (page 115) cabbage salad with jerk seasoning and nuts.

Rub the jerk seasoning into the pork. Heat the oil in a skillet over medium-high heat. Place the meat in the hot skillet and brown on both sides, cooking for approximately 3 minutes on each side. Reduce the heat and place the apple slices on top of the meat. Cover so that the heat from the pork steams the apple slices. Cook for 10 minutes.

Pour 3 tablespoons of the Tamarind-Apricot Sauce over the pork and the apples to make a glaze. Cook for 1 more minute, then turn both the apples and the meat and cook on the other side for 1 more minute. Serve with the remaining sauce and pan drippings.

YIELD: 4 SERVINGS

Jerked Pork Chops & Fruited Rice Pilaf

4 lean pork chops, about ½ inch thick

4 teaspoons Dry Jerk Seasoning (page 16)

¾ cup uncooked white rice

¼ cup sliced scallions (keep white and green parts separate)

1 (17-ounce) can chunky mixed fruit or fruit cocktail

1 cup chicken broth

2 teaspoons lime juice

Add a salad for an easy to prepare meal.

Sprinkle the chops with the Dry Jerk Seasoning, using approximately 1 teaspoon for all 4 pork chops. Brown on each side in a lightly greased ovenproof skillet. Remove the chops. Add the rice and white part of the scallions. Add the remaining 3 teaspoons jerk seasoning. Cook until golden brown.

Preheat the oven to 350° F.

Drain the fruit and reserve the syrup. Stir the broth, ¾ cup of the reserved syrup, and the lime juice into the rice. Place the chops over the rice mixture. Cover and bake for 20 minutes. Stir in the fruit and green scallion tops. Taste and adjust the seasonings, if necessary. Replace the cover and continue baking for 15 minutes. Fluff the rice lightly with a fork and serve.

YIELD: 4 SERVINGS

Pork & Mango Curry

3 tablespoons all-purpose
   flour
1½-pound pork tenderloin,
   cut into 1-inch cubes
2 tablespoons vegetable oil
1 onion, thickly sliced
2 small red or green
   bell peppers, sliced
1 tablespoon curry powder
2 tablespoons Dry Jerk
   Seasoning or to taste
   (page 16)
1 very small knuckle
   (about 1 inch) fresh
   ginger root, grated
1 (16-ounce) can tomatoes
2 teaspoons tomato paste
1½ cups chicken stock or
   broth
1½ pounds potatoes,
   peeled and cubed
2 large ripe mangoes,
   peeled, pitted, and sliced

This curry was developed by the East Indians who were brought to Jamaica in the mid-1800s as indentured servants. The recipe combines jerk seasoning with curry powder.

Place the flour in a plastic bag and add the pork cubes. Toss to coat the meat with the flour.

Heat the oil in a Dutch oven. Add the pork and sauté for approximately 5 minutes. Add the onion and bell peppers and sauté for 3 more minutes. Stir in the curry, Dry Jerk Seasoning, and ginger. Cook and stir constantly for 1 minute. Add the tomatoes, tomato paste, stock, and potatoes. Stir well to mix, then cook for 15 minutes over low heat. Add the mango slices and continue to cook until the potatoes are tender, 20 to 25 minutes. Serve with rice, boiled green bananas, chutney, and fried plantains.

YIELD: 6 SERVINGS

Smoked Fresh Ham

1 fresh ham or Boston butt
  (6 to 8 pounds)
1 recipe Jerk Rub
  (page 14)
2 cups chablis or other dry
  white wine
1 (46-ounce) can
  unsweetened pineapple
  juice
½ cup lemon juice

If you use a Boston butt, you will have a meat that is very much like an American barbecue. It is wonderful with the traditional American accompaniments—deviled eggs, baked beans, potato salad, and corn on the cob. Jamaican accompaniments would be roasted breadfruit and a mango salad.

Smoked meat freezes very well. When I go to the effort to stoke up the smoker, I usually fill it with as much meat as I can get in it.

Evenly coat the meat with the Jerk Rub. Mix the wine, pineapple juice, and lemon juice, and set aside.

Prepare a charcoal fire in the smoker and let it burn for 10 to 15 minutes. Place the water pan in the smoker, and fill with the pineapple juice mixture. Add enough hot water to fill the pan if necessary.

Place the food in the smoker according to the manufacturer's directions. Cover with the smoker lid and cook for about 3½ hours. Remove the lid and turn the meat. Baste with drippings from the drip pan. If necessary, add more liquid to the water pan. Cover the meat as quickly as possible and continue to cook for 2 to 3 hours, or until done.

Serve hot, if you can. Many people say smoked ham is not as good reheated and will serve leftovers at room temperature. The meat can be sliced or chipped.

YIELD: 12 TO 14 SERVINGS

Feathered Friends

Authentic Jamaican Jerk Chicken

David's Jerk Chicken

Jamaican Jerk Chicken Breasts

Barbecued Chicken

Jerk Cornish Hens

Caribbean Roasted Chicken on a
    Vertical Roaster

Island Glazed Chicken

Simmered Jerk Chicken

Baked Jerk Chicken Wings

Jerk Chicken Stir Fry

Caribbean Chicken Salad

Spicy Chicken Salad in a Pineapple Shell

In Jamaica when I was a little girl, Sunday dinner was often a roast chicken that was laced with cracked pimento and scallions. At that time we did not know the flavoring combination was jerk! But we loved it.

And my, those chickens were tasty—not like the poorly flavored supermarket chickens I buy these days. You see, every year for Easter, my Grandma Hulda, who was raised in the country, gave each grandchild half a dozen multicolored chickens to raise. Then Grandma Hulda would bring another half dozen hens to the laying coop as well. Every morning we would go out and pick the warm eggs from our own chickens. When the hens became too old to lay, then they became Sunday dinner in some form—a roast, a delicious chicken fricassee, or soup.

So we all grew up with chicken—except for when the mongoose would get in the coop and kill the hens. Mongooses were brought from India or Africa to the sugar plantations to keep the snakes out, but they later became quite a nuisance as they multiplied and multiplied. It became quite a feat for my grandmother to figure out how to keep the mongooses from her chickens. Mesh wire was everywhere. She would even lay traps for the mongooses; Grandma Hulda was a mean old lady, I tell you!

Authentic Jamaican Jerk Chicken

2 chickens (approximately
  3½ pounds each) cut into
  serving pieces
1½ cups Jerk Marinade
  (page 15)

Rub the chicken with the marinade and marinate in the refrigerator for at least 4 hours.

For authentic flavor, build a fire in the grill with a combination of coals and allspice (pimento) wood. If you don't have allspice wood, substitute apple wood or hickory, or build a fire with charcoal. Place the chicken pieces on the grill over white hot coals, skin side down. This will grease the grill and prevent the chicken from sticking. Baste frequently and turn the chicken every 10 minutes or so. Over a slow fire, which is preferred, the chicken will cook in approximately 1½ to 2 hours. Over a hotter grill, the chicken will take 30 to 40 minutes. The chicken is done when the flesh feels firm and the juices run clear when the meat is pricked with a fork.

YIELD: 6 SERVINGS

David's Jerk Chicken

½ cup commercially pre-
  pared or homemade
  Jerk Rub (page 14)
1 onion, finely chopped
1 fresh hot pepper or 2
  tablespoons hot pepper
  sauce
1 sprig fresh thyme, finely
  chopped
2 scallions, finely chopped
1 chicken (3 to 3½ pounds)
  cut in to serving pieces

In the parish of St. Ann, the garden parish of Jamaica, live my very good friends David and Eli Rickham, owners of a wonderful pimento plantation, Sussex Estate. They live way up on a rugged hilltop, and from their house, overlooking acres and acres of pimento trees, which yield the main ingredient in jerk seasoning, is a magnificent view of the harbor. I have been there many times for Sunday lunch, which is a big event in Jamaica, and enjoyed David's Jerk Chicken.

David's Jerk Chicken is a very special concoction. He starts with a prepared jerk sauce, which one can buy at a supermarket. Then he adds his own ingredients to make it exactly as he wants it: a little more chopped green onion, some more thyme, more hot pepper. Finally, he sniffs and says, "Aha! This is it." He knows he has the right mix just by smelling the spices and seeing the consistency he likes. He rubs his chicken with the spice mix and lets it marinate for at least 4 hours before putting it on his grill, which burns a combination of coals and pimento wood.

There are a few jerk seasoning pastes and rubs available in specialty food stores. If you can't find one locally, check the mail order suppliers listed at the back of this book.

Mix together the jerk seasoning, onion, hot pepper sauce, thyme, and scallions. Rub the chicken well with the jerk paste. Allow to marinate for at least 4 hours in the refrigerator.

Prepare a fire in the grill using a combination of coals and pimento wood. If you don't have pimento wood, substitute apple wood or hickory, or build a fire with just charcoal.

Place the chicken on the grill over white hot coals. Jerk (cook) over a very slow fire for 1 to 1½ hours, turning every 10 minutes or so. The chicken takes on a very dark color when done. David's Jerk Chicken is cooked over an open fire with the grill at a height of about 1½ feet above the fire. At no point is his grill closed.

YIELD: 6 SERVINGS

Jamaican Jerk Chicken Breasts

4 large chicken breasts, split, with bone in
2 to 3 teaspoons Jerk Rub (page 14)

White meat has a tendency to dry out on the grill, so these breasts are first baked slowly in the oven. Then they are finished on the grill to give them a crisp coating.

Wash the breasts thoroughly. Remove the skin if desired. Smear with the Jerk Rub (apply a thin coating for medium heat, a thick coating for hotter flavor). Place in a buttered glass dish, cover, and marinate in the refrigerator for 2 to 3 hours.

Preheat the oven to 275° F., then bake the breasts, covered, for 30 minutes. Meanwhile, prepare a hot fire in the barbecue grill. Remove the breasts from the oven and immediately place them on the grill, skin side down. Grill for 5 minutes on each side, or until the skin is crispy.

YIELD: 4 SERVINGS

Barbecued Chicken

½ cup cooking oil
1 cup cider vinegar
2 tablespoons Dry Jerk
   Seasoning or more to
   taste (page 16)
¼ teaspoon ground white
   pepper
1 raw egg
5 chicken broiler halves

This sauce offers just the suggestion of jerk flavor. For more spice, generously sprinkle more Dry Jerk Seasoning over the chicken as it cooks.

I like to serve barbecued chicken with Jamaican Cole Slaw (page 115) and French fries sprinkled with Dry Jerk Seasoning (page 16).

Prepare a fire in the grill using a combination of coals and pimento wood. If you don't have pimento wood, substitute apple wood or hickory, or build a fire with just charcoal.

Mix all the ingredients, except the chicken, in a blender to make the barbecue sauce. Set aside.

Wash the chicken, pat dry, and place on the grill over white hot coals, skin side down. Grill for 20 minutes per side, basting frequently with the sauce. For more flavor, sprinkle generously with additional Dry Jerk Seasoning.

YIELD: 5 SERVINGS

Jerk Cornish Hens

4 Cornish hens (1½ pounds each)
2 tablespoons cooking oil
3 tablespoons Dry Jerk Seasoning (page 16)
Honey-Ginger Dipping Sauce (page 118)

Dry Jerk Seasoning gives a light flavoring to the delicate taste of the Cornish hen.

If you are using bamboo skewers, soak them in water for 20 to 30 minutes to keep them from charring. Prepare fire in the grill.

Remove the backbone from the hens by hitting the backbone hard with the side of a large knife or cleaver; this should crack the bone. Then flatten the bird with your hand and cut away the backbone. Spread the two halves out and press down on the breastbone to flatten. Insert 1 skewer through the wings and breast and 1 skewer through the legs to keep the hens flat.

Coat the hens with oil to keep their moisture in, then with the Dry Jerk Seasoning. Place them on the grill over white hot coals, skin side down. Cook until the juices run clear when the meat is pierced, 25 to 35 minutes, brushing the hens with the dipping sauce and turning them 2 or 3 times during cooking. Serve hot, passing additional dipping sauce at the table.

YIELD: 4 SERVINGS

Caribbean Roasted Chicken on a Vertical Roaster

3½-pound roasting chicken
6 teaspoons Dry Jerk
  Seasoning (page 16)
½ cup Honey-Ginger
  Dipping Sauce (page
  118)

A great low-fat way to cook chicken is to use a vertical roaster or a rotisserie, which are available at most kitchen supply stores. Using one makes a crisper chicken since it allows all the fat to drain out. The chicken cooks faster, too, because it is in a free-standing, vertical position.

Preheat the oven to 350° F.

Rub the cavity of the chicken with 2 teaspoons of the Dry Jerk Seasoning. Use your finger or the point of a knife to loosen the chicken skin surrounding the breastbone and put 2 teaspoons of the seasoning directly on the breast of the chicken. Rub 2 teaspoons of the seasoning over the exterior of the chicken.

Place the chickens on the vertical roaster and place the roaster in another pan to catch the drips. Roast for 45 minutes. If you are not using a vertical roaster, roast for 20 minutes per pound (about 1¼ hours).

Cut the chicken into serving pieces, then drizzle each piece with some dipping sauce. Serve hot.

YIELD: 4 SERVINGS

Island Glazed Chicken

1 chicken (3 to 4 pounds)
1 tablespoon Jerk Rub
  (page 14)
1 cup Passion Fruit Sauce
  (page 146)

W ho would ever have thought that passion fruit would go with jerk seasoning? I assure you, it is great; the sweet and tangy passion fruit sauce balances the fiery flavor of the jerk.

Split the chicken down the back and flatten. Rub the meat with the Jerk Rub and marinate in the refrigerator for at least 1 hour.

Preheat the oven to 375°F., then roast the chicken, uncovered, for 45 minutes. Pour the Passion Fruit Sauce over the chicken and continue roasting for 30 minutes, or until the juices run clear when the chicken is pierced with a fork at its thickest part. Cut into serving pieces and serve.

YIELD: 4 TO 5 SERVINGS

Simmered Jerk Chicken

1 cup water
½ cup soy sauce (I use a
 low-sodium brand)
2 tablespoons sugar
2 tablespoons rum or
 sherry
2 onions, chopped
2 anise seeds (optional, but
 it does give a marvelous
 flavor)
4 teaspoons Dry Jerk
 Seasoning (page 16) or 2
 teaspoons Jerk Rub
 (page 14)
1 broiler chicken (3 to 4
 pounds) skinned and cut
 into serving pieces
1 (4-ounce) can sliced
 water chestnuts

I have been cooking this dish for over 20 years; it is a favorite of my children. Not only is it delicious, it freezes very well.

Combine the water, soy sauce, sugar, rum, onions, and anise seeds in a Dutch oven and bring to a boil. Stir in the jerk seasoning or paste; then add the chicken. The mixture should barely cover the chicken. Bring to a boil, reduce the heat, and simmer for 15 to 20 minutes with the cover on. Remove the cover, turn the chicken to allow for even cooking, and simmer over medium heat for about 20 minutes. Add the water chestnuts and cook for 1 to 2 minutes more. Before serving, skim off any fat. Serve with boiled rice.

YIELD: 4 SERVINGS

Baked Jerk Chicken Wings

12 to 18 chicken wings
  or 12 drumsticks
1½ cups Jerk Marinade
  (page 15)
1½ cups Tamarind-
  Apricot Sauce
  (page 120)
¼ cup soy sauce

A delicious variation on Buffalo wings.

Combine the chicken with the marinade and marinate in the refrigerator for 1½ hours, turning occasionally. The longer the chicken marinates, the hotter it becomes. Remove the chicken from the marinade, saving the marinade for basting.

Preheat the oven to 350° F. Place the chicken in a greased baking dish. Bake for 40 to 45 minutes, basting twice with the leftover marinade.

Prepare a dipping sauce by combining the Tamarind-Apricot Sauce with the soy sauce. Serve the chicken hot or at room temperature with the dipping sauce.

YIELD: 4 TO 6 SERVINGS AS AN APPETIZER; 2 TO 3 SERVINGS AS A
        MAIN COURSE

Jerk Chicken Stir Fry

¼ cup teriyaki sauce
(available where
Oriental foods are sold)
2 tablespoons water
1 tablespoon dry sherry or
Chinese cooking wine
1 teaspoon cornstarch
2 tablespoons vegetable oil
1 pound sliced, boned
chicken breast, cut into
1½-inch pieces
1 medium-sized onion,
chopped
2 teaspoons Dry Jerk
Seasoning or more to
taste (page 16)
½ cup green peas

Combine the teriyaki sauce, water, sherry, and cornstarch in a small bowl and set aside.

Heat the oil in a large skillet or wok. Add the chicken and onion and stir-fry until the chicken is slightly brown and the onion is just golden. Season to taste with the Dry Jerk Seasoning. Add the peas, then the teriyaki sauce mix. Cook until the sauce has thickened slightly. Serve hot with boiled rice.

YIELD: 4 SERVINGS

Caribbean Chicken Salad

3 boneless whole chicken
  breasts
2 tablespoons Jerk
  Marinade (page 15)
½ cup chopped celery
1 cup fresh pineapple, cut
  into bite-sized chunks,
  or 1 (20-ounce) can
  pineapple chunks in
  juice
2 tablespoons mayonnaise
1 cup finely shredded
  lettuce

Plan ahead and save yourself a little preparation time: Cook several extra chicken breasts on the grill with jerk seasoning and use them later in this delicious salad!

If the chicken breasts are not already cooked, preheat the oven to 350° F. Arrange the chicken breasts in a large pan and pour the marinade over them. Bake for 20 to 25 minutes, or until done. Remove from the oven and cool.

Cut or shred the chicken breasts into small pieces and put into a medium-sized bowl. Mix in the celery, pineapple, and mayonnaise. Serve on a bed of lettuce.

You can serve at once, but I prefer this salad well chilled.

YIELD: 6 SERVINGS

Spicy Chicken Salad in a Pineapple Shell

1 pineapple
¼ cup Jerk Marinade (page 15)
¼ cup Honey-Ginger Dipping Sauce (page 118)
1 teaspoon cooking oil
1 tablespoon chopped scallion
12 ounces broiled or grilled chicken breasts or thighs, diced
¼ cup coarsely chopped roasted cashews

For festive occasions, this chicken salad looks smashing in the pineapple shell.

Slice the pineapple in half lengthwise. Scoop out the center of each half, reserving the shells and discarding the tough pulp. Dice the remaining fruit.

In a bowl, combine the marinade, dipping sauce, oil, and scallion. Add the diced chicken, diced pineapple, and cashews. Mix well until all the ingredients are well coated. Serve in the pineapple shells.

You may serve the salad at once, but I prefer to serve it well chilled.

YIELD: 2 SERVINGS

Seafood Sampler

Miss Emma's Jerked Fish

Independence Day Grilled Red Snapper

Jerked Oriental Grilled Red Snapper

Caribbean Salmon Steaks

Jerk Lobster with Butter Sauce

Grilled Shrimp

Island Shrimp

Jerked Lobster with Coconut

Jerked Scallops

Broiled Jerk Snapper Fillet

Steamed Fish

Steamed Yellowfin Dolphin

Escovitch Fish

Fried Snapper with Onions

Shrimp Salad with Fresh Papaya

Codfish & Ackee

Fish Tea

Fish has always been an important part of our diet. It must be *fresh, fresh* fish, as it was when I was growing up and refrigerators were small and freezers were definitely not part of the Jamaican household.

Buying fish was always an experience. My father and I would drive out about 20 miles from Kingston on a Saturday morning at dawn in the cool morning breeze to wait for the fishermen coming in with their wonderful catch of snapper, goat fish, parrot fish, kingfish, and sprats. We would watch the sun come up and laugh and chat with the others who were waiting on the fishermen.

Finally, there would come the boats! As the fishermen pulled up the nets, we could see the beautiful colors of the fish, so fresh that they were still jumping and flipping in the nets. In the early morning sun, it was always a sight to see—the reds and oranges of the snappers, the brilliant blue of the parrot fish. And then there were the conversations to hear!

Mr. Fisherman:	Lawd, what a way de fish dem pretty today.
Buyer:	Give me two of those pretty snappers.
Mr. Fisherman:	Which ones?
Buyer:	How you mean which ones?! See those two jumping there?

[*Mind you, practically the entire catch was still jumping!*]

I want to jerk them for lunch today. Also give me three parrot fish—none with too many bones!

Mr. Fisherman:	You ever hear my parrot fish have bones yet??

[*The parrot fish is a beautiful brilliant blue and delicious, but as bony a fish as you will ever find.*]

And so it went. We would have a wonderful morning and be back home before nine.

Those who were not able to go directly to the boats could buy from fish vendors who bought from the fishermen and then peddled to the households. What ingenious carts they developed! Their pushcarts were made of wood, maybe 5 feet by 3 feet with a steering wheel salvaged from an old car and mounted at the back. The steering wheel was usually connected to the front wheels with a bike chain and some rope. The front wheels were made from metal bearings and were covered with strips of old car tires (with treads where possible!). With a horizontal bar across his lower back, the fish man was able to push a step with his right and ride with his left and then push with his left and ride with his right. It was a jump-on, jump-off motion, just as you see children here maneuvering on a scooter. Mind you, these carts were very heavy by the time they were loaded with alternating layers of ice, burlap bags, and fish!

Every fish man had an old set of three-cornered scales that he held high with his hand to give some semblance of weighing the fish. I don't know how accurate this system was, but we all abided happily by it.

Farther out in the country, the fish man rode a bicycle with a big box attached to the back. Because he had such a long way to go, his fish was packed in dry ice. The country children thought it was a big deal to beg and beg for the tiniest sliver of his dry ice, which they would promptly rub on their skin for the tingling, burning sensation!

Because we had very small refrigerators, which were also subject to power shortages, the ice factory was very important. People would buy 50 or 100 pounds of ice at a time from the factories. What a sight it was to see the huge muscles of the ice factory men as they clumped about in their big rubber boots and wielded their enormous ice tongs. When possible we went to the ice factory in the early morning because, of course, we hated to see the ice melt so quickly in the hot Jamaica sun. But when the power went out, we all ran to the ice factory with our sheets of zinc to put over the ice for at least a little protection from the heat. Then we hurried home to chill what we could until the power came back on.

In this section, you will see many different types of fish used, and many different ways you can prepare them. The classic jerked fish that is found in the jerk huts is coated with a jerk paste and then smoked slowly over the grill along with the chicken. But you can use jerk flavors to enhance all sorts of fish dishes, including those baked in the oven and steamed on top of the stove. We also make escovitch fish, which is often served for Lent, and which is also found on every buffet table in Jamaica.

Since some of the tastiest jerk recipes require cooking fish on a grill, let me first recommend that you get a basket for your grill. There are many sizes and shapes of grill baskets—some simple rectangles, some elaborately fish shaped. I prefer the simple rectangular basket, since it will hold the widest variety of cuts and types of fish and shellfish. Using a basket will truly simplify your grilling of fish. No more fish slipping around on the grill when you are trying to turn it! Do be sure, however, to grease the basket thoroughly or to spray it with a nonstick spray oil. You don't want the fish sticking to either the basket or the grill.

Next, the most important consideration in cooking fish of any type is selecting fish that is fresh. You may not be able to buy your fish directly off the boat, but do remember that freshness is more important than anything else in buying fish! Always check their eyes, yes, their eyes.

When buying whole fish, the eyes should be crystal clear and bright. The gills should still show a little red underneath. The skin should be fresh and shiny. The flesh should feel firm and elastic enough to spring back when pressed with your finger. There should be no smell other than a slight seaweed odor.

When buying steaks and fillets, look for flesh that is firm and moist to the touch. The color should be translucent, not white (a sign of age). If you notice a slimy film on the fish, it is too old.

Grilled fish cooks quickly. A whole fish will cook in 8 to 10 minutes per side, and fillets will cook in 4 to 5 minutes per side. Since you don't want to char the fish, the coals should have burned down to white ash. Because fish easily falls apart, even in a basket, I turn my fish only once during cooking—even if it is *jerked* fish.

This is not a time to leave the grill—fish cooks very quickly and tastes much better when it is light and tender. Remember too that the fish will continue to cook a little after you remove it from the grill.

If you should happen to be in Jamaica, I recommend you try the jerked fish at Miss Emma's jerk stand. The stand is located on a secluded, unpaved road used by locals to get from Kingston to Ocho Rios. The road will shake your entrails out to travel on it! But, it's worth it all to find Miss Emma's.

From the looks of it, Miss Emma's is the usual jerk pit with the requisite few tables and chairs, as well as the usual rum, reggae music, sunshine, domino games, and laughter. Miss Emma is a large lady, not in the sense of being fat but in the sense of having a very firm presence. Her age is hard to reckon—anywhere from 40 to 65—but she has not lost any of her sex appeal. Miss Emma's welcoming smile makes you feel good just to be there.

The people who come to Miss Emma's enjoy their jerk with a liberal helping of politics when Miss Emma holds court, discussing the latest moves of the government. Truly one goes to Miss Emma's for the whole experience, not just the food.

When Miss Emma jerks fish she uses a converted oil drum rather than a pit. In this way, she can build a slightly hotter fire, which does not dry out the fish as much. Her fish is cooked on foil to keep it from sticking, since we do not have grill baskets in Jamaica. It takes a little longer to cook a whole fish than fillets, but I prefer it this way, because it keeps the flesh of the fish more intact and less dried out. In fact, Miss Emma never jerks fillets at all, just fresh whole fish. The recipe that follows comes as close as possible to replicating Miss Emma's jerked fish. You must add the sunshine and music.

Miss Emma's Jerked Fish

1 tablespoon Jerk Rub
   (page 14)
1 whole red snapper
   (3 to 4 pounds), gutted
   with head left on

While many Americans are a little squeamish about seeing a fish with a head still on it, remember that keeping the head on during preparation and cooking will help retain the natural moisture of the fish.

This is delicious served with roasted sweet potatoes or johnny cakes. At Miss Emma's it is served with bammy (see page 103) or festival (see page 107). I hope you will try them too! And then share your meal with lots of friends and drink plenty of Red Stripe beer.

Prepare a fire in the grill. Massage the Jerk Rub into the fish and allow to set for a few minutes. Cook over white hot coals for 8 to 10 minutes per side. Be careful not to overcook so the fish doesn't dry out. Serve hot with a slice or two of bammy and a few slices of avocado.

YIELD: 4 SERVINGS

Independence Day Grilled Red Snapper

1 cup Dry Jerk Seasoning
  (page 16)
2 cups white wine
2 tablespoons oil
3 red snappers (3 pounds
  each) gutted, with heads
  and tails left on

On August 6, 1962, Jamaica became independent from Great Britain. The newness of this event makes it a very special holiday to all Jamaicans.

The month leading up to August 6 is always buzzing with activity. We have floats and parades, and the children in school are encouraged to create works of art, sewing, and poetry in honor of our independence. There are music competitions and, of course, culinary competitions.

In honor of Independence Day, I always stage a barbecue in Kingston where I grew up, in the backyard, under the almond tree and Bombay mango tree. These trees are as old as our Independence Day celebration itself and have hosted many luncheons and picnics. It is a time of family and close friends coming together. Children frolic on the grass, teenagers play games and flirt, and the adults reminisce.

The menu is extensive and always includes this recipe for grilled snapper. To cook the fish on the grill, I oil a grill basket and grill the fish in the basket, which will keep the fish from sticking and falling apart.

Mix together the Dry Jerk Seasoning, white wine, and oil. Set the fish in a flat dish and pour the jerk and wine mixture over top. Let the fish marinate for about 1 hour in the refrigerator. Meanwhile, prepare a fire in the grill.

Grill over white hot coals for 8 to 10 minutes a side. Serve hot, with Rice and Peas (page 112) and a tossed salad.

YIELD: 10 TO 12 SERVINGS

Jerked Oriental Grilled Red Snapper

4 scallions, diced
3 garlic cloves, diced
2 tablespoons Jerk Rub
   (page 14)
Zest of 2 lemons
2 red snappers (about 2
   pounds each) gutted
   with heads left on
¼ cup lemon juice
2 tablespoons soy sauce
2 tablespoons olive oil

Almost any grilled fish recipe can be adapted to jerk cooking, even those with distinctive seasonings of their own. In this recipe, I started with my favorite recipe for grilled red snapper, which is seasoned with garlic, ginger, and soy sauce. I replaced the ginger with Jerk Rub and voila! Jerked Oriental Grilled Red Snapper. You can do the same with your favorite recipes.

Incidentally, a lot of Jamaican cooking borrows from the Orient for the simple reason that in our melting pot of cultures, many people of Oriental descent have settled here.

Prepare a fire in the grill, and be sure to grease the grid itself.

Mix the scallions, half the garlic, 1 tablespoon of the Jerk Rub, and the lemon zest in a bowl. Spread half of this mixture inside each of the snappers. Mix together the remaining garlic and 1 tablespoon Jerk Rub, as well as the lemon juice, soy sauce, and olive oil as a baste for the fish.

When the coals are white hot, place the fish on the grill. Baste several times during cooking. Grill the fish until just done, 8 to 10 minutes a side. Serve hot with rice.

YIELD: 4 TO 6 SERVINGS

Caribbean Salmon Steaks

About 2 teaspoons
   vegetable oil for each
   steak
Salmon steaks, about 2
   inches thick
Dry Jerk Seasoning
   (page 16) to taste

These steaks should be served with the Honey-Ginger Dip-ping Sauce (page 118). This is delicious with corn on the cob and Jamaican Cole Slaw (page 115). You can substitute kingfish steaks for the salmon.

Prepare a fire in the grill.

Rub the oil liberally over the salmon steaks. Sprinkle the Dry Jerk Seasoning over the salmon steaks as if it were salt and pepper. Place the seasoned steaks in a well-greased basket over the hot coals. Grill for 5 to 6 minutes on either side, being careful not to overcook. When the fish flakes just slightly, it is done. Remember that it will continue to cook so you may want to take it off the grill when it is slightly underdone. Serve hot.

Jerk Lobster with Butter Sauce

Butter Sauce
½ cup butter
1 scallion, including green top, thinly sliced
2 teaspoons lime juice or to taste
2 to 3 drops hot pepper sauce, preferably Scotch bonnet pepper sauce, or to taste

Lobster
4 rock lobster tails (7 to 8 ounces each)
2 tablespoons melted butter
1 teaspoon Jerk Rub (page 14)

T he spicy butter sauce is wonderful with many different types of seafood.

Prepare a fire in the grill.

While the coals burn down, make the Butter Sauce by melting the butter in a small saucepan. Add the scallion and sauté lightly until just golden. Add the lime juice and hot pepper sauce to taste. Set aside.

To prepare the lobster tails, cut the top membrane with kitchen shears and discard. Use your hand to loosen the meat from the shell, leaving the tail section attached. Brush each tail with melted butter and approximately ¼ teaspoon of Jerk Rub.

When the coals are whitish gray, grease the grill and place the tails meat side down. Cook for 2 to 3 minutes. Turn the tails over and continue cooking until done, approximately 7 to 9 minutes. By cooking the lobster with the shell side down most of the time, you will help preserve its natural juices. The lobster is done when it turns opaque. Don't worry if the shell chars.

If you prefer, you can broil the lobster in the oven. Broil the tails, meat side down, for 2 to 3 minutes. Then turn and broil for about 4 minutes more.

Serve immediately with the Butter Sauce and garlic bread, or with Baked Breadfruit (page 109).

YIELD: 4 SERVINGS

Grilled Shrimp

2 pounds large shrimp (16 to 20 count) cleaned, shelled, and deveined
Vegetable oil
Dry Jerk Seasoning (page 16) to taste

S hrimp cooked on a grill is delicious—you may also want to cook a few extra to have for Shrimp Salad with Fresh Papaya (page 77).

Prepare a fire in the grill. The shrimp can be grilled on skewers or in a double-hinged grill basket. If you use bamboo skewers, be sure to soak them in water for 20 to 30 minutes before using them to keep them from catching on fire. If you plan to use a grill basket, be sure to grease it.

Brush the shrimp with a little oil, then sprinkle on the Dry Jerk Seasoning as you would use salt and pepper.

Cook on the grill for approximately 3 to 4 minutes on each side. Don't leave the grill unattended as shrimp are easy to overcook.

Serve hot, perhaps with roasted plantain and an avocado salad. Remember that you can always rub oil on a plantain and wrap it in foil to bake while you prepare your seafood. A simple pasta dish is also very good with the Grilled Shrimp.

YIELD: 5 TO 6 SERVINGS

Island Shrimp

1 to 1¼ pounds large
 shrimp (16 to 20 count)
1 (12-ounce) bottle Red
 Stripe beer
¼ cup Key West lime juice
2 teaspoons Dry Jerk
 Seasoning (page 16)
¾ cup Honey-Ginger
 Dipping Sauce
 (page 118)

I know it is a pain to have recipes specify brand name ingredients that may not be found in your local supermarket. But for true Jamaican flavor, you must use these brand name items. For delicious flavor that is not authentic, your local sources will be fine.

The shrimp can be grilled, broiled, or cooked in a stove-top smoker, if you are lucky enough to have one. The shrimp will cook in 10 to 15 minutes in a stove-top smoker, and can be given a boost of extra flavor with 2 teaspoons of mesquite smoke dust, which is available where barbecue supplies are sold.

This recipe was developed by Kitchenique in Destin, Florida.

Prepare a fire in the grill if needed. Rinse the shrimp and devein, leaving the shell on the shrimp.

Combine the beer, lime juice, and Dry Jerk Seasoning in a bowl and add the shrimp. Marinate for about 5 minutes. Place the shrimp in a greased grill basket and grill over white hot coals for about 5 minutes, turning once; or broil for 3 to 5 minutes, turning once. Check for doneness, then serve with the dipping sauce.

YIELD: 3 TO 4 SERVINGS

Jerked Lobster with Coconut

½ cup milk

1 cup unsweetened cream of coconut (available where Hispanic foods are sold)

2 tablespoons Dry Jerk Seasoning (page 16)

Meat of 4 medium-sized lobsters, shelled and cut into chunks

Salt and pepper to taste

¼ cup freshly grated Parmesan cheese

8 toast points

The flavor of jerk is delicious mixed with coconut. The sweetness of the coconut balances well with the spiciness of the jerk. You will find this a wonderful variation on Lobster Thermidor. It is easily made in the oven.

Preheat the oven to 400° F.

Mix together the milk and cream of coconut. Heat in a large saucepan over moderate heat. Add the Dry Jerk Seasoning. Stir and cook for about 5 minutes. Add the lobster chunks and salt and pepper to taste and reduce the heat. Simmer for 7 to 8 minutes to blend all the flavors. Pour the mixture into a baking dish and sprinkle with the grated cheese. Bake for about 15 minutes, until the lobster is browned. Serve over toast points, allowing 2 per servings. Baked potatoes and broccoli go well with this dish.

YIELD: 4 SERVINGS

Jerked Scallops

2 tablespoons butter
2 tablespoons oil
1 pound bay scallops
2 tablespoons Dry Jerk
  Seasoning (page 16)
3 tablespoons white wine

Do not leave the stove while you are cooking the scallops. It is very easy to turn scallops from a excellent offering from the sea to a pile of rubber because of overcooking. These scallops are delicious as an appetizer or as a main course.

Heat the butter and oil in a sauté pan over medium-high heat until they are blended. Add the scallops and sauté only until they change color. Then add the seasoning and the wine and quickly remove from the stove top. Serve at once.

If you are serving this as a main course, you may want to serve the scallops on a bed of rice that has been moistened with the delicious cooking liquid.

YIELD: 8 SERVINGS AS AN APPETIZER; 2 TO 3 SERVINGS AS A MAIN
       COURSE

Broiled Jerk Snapper Fillet

1 tablespoon Dry Jerk
    Seasoning (page 16)
Dash hot pepper sauce,
    preferably Scotch
    bonnet pepper sauce
2 tablespoons oil or
    margarine
10-ounce snapper fillet

Blend the jerk seasoning, pepper sauce, and oil. Cover the fillet with the mix, being careful to coat the fillet all over. Place in a pan approximately 4 inches from the broiler. Broil until the fish flakes when tested with a fork, which will take just a few minutes. Unless the fillet is very thick, it is not necessary to turn the fish as it cooks. Serve at once with garlic bread and a green salad.

YIELD: 2 SERVINGS

Steamed Fish

2 to 2½ pounds grouper, parrot fish, or red snapper
2 tablespoons soy sauce
2 to 3 teaspoons Dry Jerk Seasoning (page 16) or to taste

In Jamaica, no one had anything as fancy as the steamers that are now available in the United States. In order to steam fish, we just used a kettle with very little water and a very tight-fitting lid. Because of the strong Oriental influence in Jamaica, steamed food of any type is very popular.

Use a steamer if you have one; otherwise, use a large saucepan or kettle with a tight-fitting lid. To use the kettle without a steamer, place approximately ½ inch of water, stock, or beer in the kettle, and bring to a low boil. Sprinkle the fish with the soy sauce and Dry Jerk Seasoning to taste. Place the fish in the kettle and let simmer for approximately 5 to 6 minutes, or until the fish flakes readily when touched with a fork.

To prepare in a steamer, place the rack in the bottom of the pan. Add water, stock, or beer and heat to a simmer. Sprinkle the fish with the soy sauce and Dry Jerk Seasoning to taste. Place the fish on the rack. Steam for approximately 5 to 6 minutes, or until the fish flakes readily when touched with a fork. Serve hot.

YIELD: 3 TO 4 SERVINGS

Steamed Yellowfin Dolphin†

2 pounds dolphin fillets or
   any other firm fish, such
   as tuna or salmon
   (allow 7 to 8 ounces per
   person)
2 tablespoons white wine
   or sherry
¾ cup Jerk Marinade
   (page 15)
½-inch cube fresh ginger
   root, mashed
1 onion, thinly sliced

† This dolphin is a *fish* not
the mammal. It is a common
fish in the Caribbean; a
colorful, feisty game fish. It
is also known as mahimahi.

Men who fish will be very fond of this recipe, where the fish is steamed in, of all things, a dishwasher. In a what?!! Yes, run through on full cycle with hot water—but, please, no soap, I beg of you! This is delicious—let your favorite fisherman try it.

The originator of this wonderful idea is Mr. Frank Bronstorff, of the Jamaican Tourist Board in Atlanta. He is both a fervent promoter of Jamaica and an avid fisherman and builder of fishing rods.

Cut the fillets into bite-sized pieces. Mix the wine with the Jerk Marinade and ginger; pour over the fillets. Allow to marinate for approximately 20 minutes.

Then spray a large sheet of heavy-duty aluminum foil with a nonstick spray oil. Drain the fish pieces and place on the foil. Cover with onion slices. Seal the foil very tightly, and place in the top rack of the dishwasher. Run through a full cycle with hot water (but no soap). Remove from the foil and serve hot.

As an alternative to the dishwasher, place the fish and a few tablespoons of the marinade on a large sheet of aluminum foil or parchment paper that has been lightly oiled. Arrange the onion over the fish. Seal the package and place in a 400° F. oven for 8 to 10 minutes. Remove from the foil or paper. Serve hot.

YIELD: 4 SERVINGS

Escovitch Fish

Fish

2 pounds fresh fish fillets
   or steaks: kingfish,
   yellowfin dolphin, or
   any other firm fish
Juice of 2 limes
Dry Jerk Seasoning
   (page 16) to taste
Cooking oil

Pickling Mixture

1 or 2 cucumbers or
   chochos, halved and cut
   into long strips
2 onions, thinly sliced
1 tablespoon whole
   Jamaican pimento
   berries (allspice berries)
1 cup vinegar (apple cider
   vinegar is
   recommended)
2 tablespoons hot pepper
   sauce, preferably Scotch
   bonnet pepper sauce
Salt

This pickled fish dish is found throughout the Caribbean.

Clean and wash the fish, then rub with lime juice and set aside to dry. Sprinkle with the Dry Jerk Seasoning on both sides.

Heat approximately 1 inch of oil in a frying pan until it smokes. Place the fish in the hot oil in a single layer—do not overlap. Reduce the heat and fry until the fish is brown on the underside, about 2 minutes. Turn and brown on the other side. When done, drain and arrange on a large platter.

Place the cucumbers, onions, allspice, vinegar, and pepper sauce in a saucepan and bring to a boil. Add salt to taste. Simmer for 2 minutes, then remove from the heat. Pour the hot pickle over the fish. Let cool, then refrigerate to marinate. The fish may be left in the pickle to marinate for up to 3 days, or it may be served while the vegetables are still crisp. Serve hot or cold.

YIELD: 4 SERVINGS

Fried Snapper with Onions

2 to 3 tablespoons Jerk
  Rub (page 14)
6 small whole snappers
  (12 to 16 ounces each),
  gutted, with heads left
  on
Oil
2 small onions, thinly
  sliced, rings separated

Massage the Jerk Rub into the fish. Pour ½ inch of oil into a frying pan and heat over medium-high heat. Add the fish and fry, turning once, until golden brown, 2 to 3 minutes per side. When you turn the fish, add the onion rings and continue to cook the fish and onions. By the time the second side of the snapper is browned, the onions should be barely softened. Remove both with a slotted spoon onto paper towels to drain. Serve hot.

YIELD: 6 SERVINGS

Shrimp Salad with Fresh Papaya

1 chocho
8 ounces shrimp, shelled, deveined, and cooked
½ cup diced celery
¼ small fresh papaya, peeled and diced, seeds removed
¼ cup mayonnaise
2 teaspoons Dry Jerk Seasoning (page 16)
2 tablespoons Passion Fruit Sauce (page 146)

The chocho featured in this recipe is known by different names in different areas and by different ethnic groups: chayote to those of Spanish heritage, *christophene* to those of French origins, chocho to those of us from Jamaica. You might also encounter it under the names mirliton or vegetable pear. The chocho is also one of our regular vegetables, which we fix in soups and serve stuffed as a main course.

The trick to having the salad seem like it contains more shrimp is to cut the chocho the same size as the shrimp. The blandness of the chocho will pick up the wonderful flavor of the shrimp. If you can't find any chochos, you can substitute 1 cucumber, peeled, seeded, and diced. Do not cook the cucumber before adding it to the salad.

Peel the chocho and then blanch in boiling water to cover until just slightly crunchy, 4 to 5 minutes. Slice in half, then remove the stringy pith in the middle. Dice to be the same size as your shrimp.

Combine the chocho, shrimp, celery, and papaya. Add the mayonnaise, jerk seasoning, and Passion Fruit Sauce. Mix thoroughly. Chill well before serving.

I like to serve this in a pineapple shell. It is very festive and tropical looking.

YIELD: 2 TO 3 SERVINGS

Codfish & Ackee

1 pound salted codfish,
   preferably boned
6 bacon strips
1 tablespoon oil
1 hot pepper, seeded and
   thinly sliced, preferably
   a Scotch bonnet
2 scallions, chopped
1 medium-sized tomato,
   diced
1 onion, chopped
1 (19-ounce) can ackees
Salt and pepper to taste
1 green bell pepper, in
   strips, for garnish

You will not be able to get fresh ackees unless you go to the islands, as there are import restrictions on this fruit. But no cookbook that deals with Jamaica would be complete without a recipe for codfish and ackee, which is almost our national dish. Canned ackees are available in ethnic food stores that specialize in Hispanic or West Indian food.

Cover the codfish with cold water and soak for 30 to 40 minutes. This will help to remove the excess salt from the fish. Pour out the original water and add another quart of fresh water. Bring to a full boil and then drain. Remove any bones and skin and then flake the codfish.

Fry the bacon in a skillet until crisp. Remove the bacon from the pan, drain well, and crumble. Set aside.

Reduce the heat under the skillet and add the oil, hot pepper, scallions, tomato, and onion. Cook until the onion is translucent, 3 to 4 minutes.

Drain the ackees and stir into the sauté mixture along with the codfish. Season to taste with salt and pepper. Cover and cook over low heat for approximately 5 minutes, or until all the flavors are blended. You will want to use a slotted spoon to remove the fish and ackees from the pan. Garnish each serving with the crumbled bacon and pepper strips.

YIELD: 6 SERVINGS

Fish Tea

8 cups cold water
2 pounds fish (heads
    or bony fish, such as
    parrot)
3 or 4 potatoes, peeled
    and cubed
1 tomato, chopped
1 sprig fresh thyme or
    1½ teaspoons dried
    thyme
½ onion, diced
1 whole hot pepper, Scotch
    bonnet if possible (must
    be unbroken)
Salt
Pepper

This wonderful light soup is almost the equivalent of America's chicken soup as far as its perceived medicinal qualities. It is frequently made with the parrot fish, which has a delicious flavor but many, many little bones. Fish Tea is usually served in a big mug or cup, not in a dainty little soup bowl.

Bring the water and fish to a boil in a soup kettle. Cover the kettle and reduce the heat to medium. Simmer for 30 minutes. Strain the stock and remove the fish.

Remove all flesh from the bones, then discard the bones. Return the fish to the broth, along with the remaining ingredients. Bring to a boil again, then reduce to a simmer. Cook until the potatoes are tender, about 20 minutes, adding more water if necessary. Remove the hot pepper without breaking it in order to get the flavor and not the heat. Serve very hot.

YIELD: 8 TO 10 SERVINGS

Here's the Beef, the Lamb & Goat

Jamaican Beef Kabobs

Grilled Rib Eyes

Caribbean Beef Filet

Stir-fried Beef

Roast Beef à la Calypso

Caribbean Burger

Beef Brisket à la Helen

Jamaican Beef Stew

Meat Loaf with Jerk

Lamb Kabobs

Lamb Fajitas

Roasted Leg of Jerked Lamb

Lamb Shank Stew

Curry Goat

Jamaican Beef Patties

In Jamaica we never had access to the better cuts of beef until 20 to 30 years ago. At that time, the American bauxite companies came to the island and developed what became our largest industry. In fact, for a long time, Jamaica was the world's largest supplier of bauxite, an ore used in the production of aluminum. Eventually, in response to demands from their transplanted employees, the bauxite companies developed cattle ranches in the plains of the island to satisfy American workers' desire for beef. You see, until then, cattle raising had been a very casual affair, with a few cows raised here and there, but hardly on a large scale or under circumstances where tenderness of beef was a goal. Consequently, we cooked only beef dishes such as stews, where the tenderness of the meat was enhanced by long, slow, moist cooking. Since then, however, we have discovered for ourselves the joys of throwing onto the grill a steak flavored with jerk seasoning and a rare roast smeared with jerk paste.

Other meats that we have long cultivated include kid and goat. It is wonderful to see all the little kid goats (called *cabaritos* by Spanish-speakers) scampering up the mountains in Jamaica—you see them everywhere! Like pigs and chickens, goats are easily grown, take up little room, and eat a variety of foods. An additional bonus of the goat is that it is a lean meat and is a good size to produce enough food for a group of 12 to 15 people. Until recently, we usually fixed curry goat, another national dish, for large parties. If you can find a source for goat, you can make curry goat for yourself!

Jamaican Beef Kabobs

3 cups Jerk Marinade
(page 15)
2 teaspoons olive oil
2-pound beef sirloin, cut
into cubes
18 small white onions,
peeled
2 medium-sized zucchini,
cut into chunks
18 medium-sized
mushrooms
18 cherry tomatoes

These kabobs are wonderful served with a pilaf or plain rice. I prefer to cook the vegetables on separate skewers, since they take less time than the beef and can turn to mush if they are overcooked.

Combine the marinade and olive oil in a resealable plastic bag. Add the meat and rotate the bag to thoroughly coat the meat. Marinate overnight or for at least several hours in the refrigerator.

Prepare a fire in the grill. If you are using bamboo skewers, soak them in water for 20 to 30 minutes to prevent charring.

Remove the meat from the bag, reserving the marinade for basting. Skewer the meat alternately with the onions. Place the zucchini, mushrooms, and cherry tomatoes on separate skewers. When the coals are red but not flaming, place the skewers on the grill about 3 inches above the coals. Grill the meat for 5 minutes on each side, turning the skewers frequently to brown the meat evenly. The vegetables should cook for 3 to 4 minutes per side. As the meat and vegetables cook, be sure to baste with the marinade; both the vegetables and the meat will acquire a delicious jerk taste. Serve hot over rice.

YIELD: 6 SERVINGS

Grilled Rib Eyes

Rib Eyes
½ cup Jerk Marinade
  (page 15)
1 tablespoon soy sauce
2 rib eye steaks (10 to 12
  ounces each)

Horseradish Sauce
½ cup heavy cream
⅓ cup mayonnaise
⅓ cup fresh grated horse-
  radish, or prepared,
  drained
1 tablespoon prepared
  mustared
½ teaspoon sugar
salt and white pepper, to
  taste

These steaks are delicious served with a creamy horseradish sauce.

Combine the Jerk Marinade and soy sauce in a resealable plastic bag. Add the steaks and rotate the bag to thoroughly coat the meat. Marinate for 1 to 2 hours in the refrigerator.

Prepare a fire in the grill. Remove the meat from the marinade and grill over hot coals for 5 minutes on each side, or until the meat is cooked to your taste. Baste occasionally. Serve hot off the grill.

YIELD: 2 SERVINGS

Caribbean Beef Filet

1 beef filet or tenderloin (1½ to 2 pounds)
Oil (I prefer corn or safflower oil, but olive oil is nice also)
5 tablespoons Dry Jerk Seasoning (page 16)

*T*his delicious "blackened" filet will make your mouth water. Developed by my husband, it is a combination of the Cajun blackened cooking technique and the wonderful flavors of the tropics. Hartmut prefers to cook the beef before it is cut into individual serving portions because it is easier to handle that way, and because the beef looks so tempting as you slice it in front of your guests! This dish is delicious served with a homemade mayonnaise seasoned with just a little Dry Jerk Seasoning and a few dashes of Scotch bonnet pepper sauce mixed in! Thinly sliced, the beef makes a delicious appetizer.

Preheat the oven to 325° F.

Coat the filet lightly with oil, then generously coat with the Dry Jerk Seasoning. I find that the neatest way to do this is to put the jerk seasoning and the oiled beef in a plastic bag and then really massage the seasoning into the beef. The oil will help hold the seasoning on the filet.

Pour 1 tablespoon of oil into an ovenproof iron skillet. Turn a stove-top burner on very high and heat oil until almost smoking. Add the filet and sear for approximately 2 minutes, turning at least once, and watching it closely. Then bake for 15 minutes, or until a meat thermometer registers 140° F. for rare. Allow the meat to rest for about 5 minutes, then slice and serve.

YIELD: 4 TO 6 SERVINGS

Stir-fried Beef

1-pound boneless round
   steak
¼ pound fresh snow peas,
   ends trimmed and
   strings removed, or 1
   (6-ounce) package
   frozen pea pods, thawed
1 carrot, sliced diagonally
1 large onion, coarsely
   chopped
1 small zucchini,
   diagonally sliced
1 tablespoon cornstarch
1½ teaspoons sugar
½ cup water
⅓ cup soy sauce
1 tablespoon dry sherry
   or Chinese rice wine
2 tablespoons vegetable oil
Dry Jerk Seasoning (page
   16) to taste (approxi-
   mately 1 tablespoon)

Jerk seasoning adds a delightful dash to this Oriental dish.

Partially freeze the steak; slice across the grain into strips that measure about 3 inches by ¼ inch; set aside. Have all the vegetables prepared. Combine the cornstarch, sugar, water, soy sauce, and sherry; set aside. Everything must be prepared before you start cooking; stir-fry cooking is very quick!

Place the oil in a preheated wok and rotate the wok to coat the sides with the oil. Heat for 2 minutes at medium-high heat. Add the beef and stir-fry until browned. Remove the beef and set aside.

Add the vegetables to the wok and stir-fry for 3 minutes, or until crisp-tender. Return the beef to the wok. Sprinkle with the Dry Jerk Seasoning and continue to stir-fry. Add the soy/cornstarch mixture to the beef. Cook, stirring constantly, until the sauce has thickened. Serve at once over hot boiled rice.

YIELD: 4 TO 6 SERVINGS

Roast Beef à la Calypso

1 cup Jerk Rub
   (page 14)
1 tablespoon vegetable oil
1 rolled rump roast (4 to
   6-pounds)

My family fights for the leftovers from this dish so they can make a variation on the French dip sandwich. What we do is mix any leftover pan juices with the Honey-Ginger Dipping Sauce on page 118 and pour that over the meat.

Combine the Jerk Rub and oil in a resealable plastic bag. Add the meat and rotate the bag to thoroughly coat the meat. Marinate overnight or for at least 5 to 6 hours in the refrigerator.

Preheat the oven to 325° F. Place the meat in a roasting pan and roast for for 2 to 2½ hours, or until a meat thermometer reaches 145° F. for rare to 170° F. for well done. Let the meat stand for about 5 minutes before slicing. Serve with the pan juices.

YIELD: 6 TO 8 SERVINGS

Caribbean Burger

1½ pounds lean ground
   beef or chuck
Dry Jerk Seasoning
   (page 16) to taste
2 tablespoons catsup
2 tablespoons Honey-
   Ginger Dipping Sauce
   (page 118)
Fresh or canned pineapple
   slices
4 to 6 hamburger buns
4 to 6 cheese slices

Season the beef with Dry Jerk Seasoning as you would salt and pepper. Form into 4 to 6 patties and cook over a prepared grill or in a skillet.

While the meat is cooking, mix the catsup with the dipping sauce. If canned pineapple is used, drain the slices. Lightly grill or heat the buns.

To serve, place the meat patties on the buns and top each with 1 slice of cheese and 1 slice of pineapple. Dress with the catsup-dipping sauce mixture. Serve at once.

YIELD: 4 TO 6 SERVINGS

Beef Brisket à la Helen

1 beef brisket (5 to 6
   pounds)
¾ cup Jerk Marinade
   (page 15)

This dish is foolproof for novices and cooks who are very busy with other things. It comes out best if you don't open the foil as the meat roasts. The meat is delicious and very tender.

Place the brisket and marinade in a resealable plastic bag and rotate the bag several times to thoroughly coat the meat. Marinate for 2 to 3 hours in the refrigerator.

Preheat the oven to 250° F. Place the brisket and marinade in a roasting pan and cover with foil. Bake for 3 to 4 hours, or until tender. Be sure to serve it with the pan drippings!

YIELD: 8 SERVINGS

Jamaican Beef Stew

1 to 2 tablespoons
vegetable oil
2-pound boneless chuck
roast, cut into 1-inch
cubes
1 quart water
1 tablespoon brown sugar
1½ teaspoons cider
vinegar
1 medium-sized onion,
sliced
1 garlic clove, minced
2 tablespoons Jerk Rub
(page 14)
4 medium-sized carrots,
cut into 2-inch chunks
4 medium-sized potatoes,
peeled and cut into
2-inch chunks
Salt and pepper to taste
1½ tablespoons cornstarch
1½ tablespoons cold water

This tasty version of beef stew is mildly flavored with Jerk Rub. If you are interested in freezing this dish, omit the potatoes, as cooked potatoes do not hold up well in the freezer. This stew is delicious cooked on top of the stove or in a Crockpot.

Heat the oil in a large Dutch oven. Add the meat and brown well. Stir in the 1 quart water, brown sugar, vinegar, onion, garlic, and Jerk Rub. Reduce the heat and simmer for 2 hours.

Add the carrots and potatoes, cover, and cook over low heat for another 20 to 30 minutes, or until the vegetables are tender. Add salt and pepper to taste.

Combine the cornstarch and the 1½ tablespoons cold water and stir until smooth. Gradually add to the stew, stirring constantly. Cook, uncovered, until the stew is thickened and bubbly, stirring frequently.

To make the stew in a Crockpot, omit the oil and reduce the water to 3 cups. Place all the ingredients in the pot except for the cornstarch/water combination. Start cooking on high, then after anywhere between 20 minutes and 2 hours, reduce the heat to low. Cook for 6 to 8 hours. (Crockpot cooking time is flexible; experiment to see what works best with your schedule.) About 20 minutes before serving, add the cornstarch/water combination as above and allow to simmer for 15 to 20 minutes to thicken the gravy.

Serve warm. This tastes even better on the second day.

YIELD: 4 TO 6 SERVINGS

Meat Loaf with Jerk

1½ pounds lean ground
  beef or ground round
2 eggs
1 large onion, finely
  chopped
1 green bell pepper, finely
  chopped
1 tablespoon Dry Jerk
  Seasoning (page 16)
1 (8-ounce) can tomato
  sauce
1 tablespoon brown sugar
1 cup cracker crumbs
  (I like the rich taste of
  Ritz or Escort crackers)

An easy dish to fix in the morning before work; just let the kids put it in the oven along with some baking potatoes when they come home from school. Presto—dinner is almost ready when you get home!

Lightly oil a 9-inch by 5-inch loaf pan. I prefer to use a spray oil. Preheat the oven to 350° F.

Mix all the ingredients together and place in the loaf pan. Smooth the top. Bake for 1 hour.

Let stand for about 15 minutes, then pour off the pan drippings and discard. Loosen the meat from the sides of the pan and invert onto a serving platter. Serve hot or cold.

YIELD: 6 SERVINGS

Lamb Kabobs

1½ cups Jerk Marinade
(page 15)
1 boneless leg of lamb (2 to
3 pounds), cubed
18 pearl onions
2 or 3 red, green, and/or
yellow bell peppers,
cubed

Although not really a traditional combination, lamb and jerk seasoning are a delicious twosome.

Combine the marinade and lamb cubes in a resealable plastic bag. Rotate the bag to coat all the meat. Marinate for 4 to 6 hours in the refrigerator.

Prepare a fire in the grill. If you are using bamboo skewers, soak them in water for 20 to 30 minutes to prevent them from charring on the grill. Alternately thread the meat, peppers, and onions on the skewers. Place the skewers in the marinade until you are ready to grill.

To grill, remove the skewers from the bag and drain well. Grill over white hot coals for 4 to 5 minutes per side, or until cooked to the desired degree of doneness, basting occasionally. Serve with rice pilaf or Baked Breadfruit (page 109).

YIELD: 6 SERVINGS

Lamb Fajitas

Fajitas

2-pound boneless shoulder
   or leg of lamb
¾ cup Jerk Marinade
   (page 15)
2 teaspoons Dry Jerk
   Seasoning (page 16)
1 large onion, sliced
2 medium-sized green bell
   peppers, cut into large
   chunks
1 tablespoon vegetable oil
1 lime
12 small flour tortillas

Condiments

Salsa
Sour cream
Guacamole
Grated cheddar cheese

This is true melting pot cookery. Mexican fajitas are one of the most popular dishes in the United States these days. This Jamaican version of fajitas combines the wonderful taste and texture of lamb with the balanced spiciness of jerk seasoning. This is also very tasty when made with flank steak.

Combine the meat and the marinade in a resealable plastic bag. Add the vegetables and marinate in the refrigerator for at least 4 hours. Remove the lamb from the bag and grill for 4 minutes on each side. Do not overcook—you will complete the cooking with the vegetables in a skillet. Remove the meat from the grill and slice thinly.

Heat the oil in a skillet or griddle and add the meat, vegetables, and Dry Jerk Seasoning. Cook quickly, just to finish cooking the meat and soften the vegetables. Squeeze lime over the mixture. Serve immediately on heated flour tortillas with salsa, sour cream, guacamole, and cheddar cheese. This is a fun dish to serve to friends. Delicious with Red Stripe beer and plenty of music!

YIELD: 4 TO 6 SERVINGS

Roasted Leg of Jerked Lamb

½ leg of lamb with bone in
(7 to 8 pounds)
4 to 6 garlic cloves
1 tablespoon olive oil
5 tablespoons Dry Jerk
Seasoning (page 16)
1 cup hot beef broth
¼ cup red wine
Salt and pepper
Honey-Ginger Dipping
Sauce (page 118)
optional

For this recipe, the oregano, thyme, and marjoram that normally season roast lamb are replaced with a jerk blend.

Preheat the oven to 450° F. Cut small slits in the surface of the leg of lamb and stud with the garlic cloves. Rub the outside of the leg of lamb with the oil. Coat heavily with the Dry Jerk Seasoning, massaging as much seasoning into the meat as you can. Place in a roasting pan.

Roast for 20 minutes; then reduce the temperature to 350° F. and continue to roast for about 1 hour, or until a meat thermometer inserted into the thickest part of the meat registers 145° F. for medium rare or 165° F. for well done.

Remove the meat to a platter and allow it to rest for 5 to 10 minutes before slicing. While the meat rests, pour the broth and wine into the roasting pan. Bring to a boil over medium heat and cook, stirring up the browned bits from the bottom of the pan, until the volume has reduced by about one third and the juices have a syrupy consistency. Season to taste with the salt and pepper. Slice the meat and serve with the pan juices and the Honey-Ginger Dipping Sauce.

YIELD: 6 TO 8 SERVINGS

Lamb Shank Stew

4 to 6 lamb shanks
1 tablespoon Jerk Rub
  (page 14)
1 large onion, coarsely
  chopped
4 large carrots
2 tablespoons tomato paste
1 (8-ounce) can tomato
  sauce

Not only are lamb shanks very economical, they are also among the most flavorful of the cuts of lamb. This is a complete meal when cooked in the Crockpot with carrots and onions. I also like it with roasted potatoes, although sometimes I add the potatoes along with the other ingredients.

Trim any excess fat from the lamb shanks. Place the meat in a Crockpot and top with the Jerk Rub. Add the remaining ingredients and turn the Crockpot on high. Cook on high for 30 to 45 minutes, then reduce the heat to low and cook for 8 hours. What a wonderful dish to greet you and the family when you come home from work! Delicious with garlic bread and a salad.

YIELD: 4 SERVINGS

Curry Goat

2 pounds goat meat
1 large onion, chopped
1 garlic clove, minced
1 hot pepper, chopped
   and seeded (or not,
   depending on how hot
   you want it)
2 tablespoons curry
   powder
Salt and pepper to taste
2 tablespoons vegetable oil
2 cups water

Curry Goat is one of our national dishes. We always serve it for our special occasions, and it seems to be one of the best-remembered dishes by tourists. Certainly it is one of the dishes I am frequently asked about by Americans who have traveled to Jamaica. As to where you will find goat meat, it will take some searching. Call around to local specialty butchers and farmers. Bear in mind that the kid goat is a bony little animal and the dish will include many bones.

Trim any fat from the goat and then cut the meat into bite-sized pieces. Don't worry about the bones; they will become soft and chewable after cooking. Combine the meat with the onion, garlic, hot pepper, curry powder, and salt and pepper in a resealable plastic bag and let stand in the refrigerator for 1 hour.

Heat the oil in a skillet over medium heat and brown the meat and vegetables until evenly cooked. Add the water, cover, and simmer for 1 hour. Correct the seasonings and add more water if needed. Continue to cook until the meat and bones are tender, 20 to 25 minutes more, depending on the tenderness of the meat.

Serve over white rice with green bananas, fried plantains, and chutney, or anything you like! You can also add potatoes or tomatoes to the curry as it cooks.

YIELD: 4 SERVINGS

Jamaican Beef Patties

~~~~~~

This wonderful meat pie, which is called an empanada by Hispanics, is a dish no Jamaican cookbook can forget. Along with jerk and bammy, beef patties are essential to the Jamaican way of life.

Patties are not a special treat; they are eaten every day, much as the hamburger is in America. Patties are eaten by the rich and the poor, by children and by old people. They are eaten in offices, served as lunch, a snack, or dinner. Interestingly, patties are rarely *made* at home. It seems that one is always standing in line at the patty stand waiting for one that is fresh and hot. Depending on the popularity of the patty shop at the moment, the line can reach all the way around the building! We visit with one another while waiting our turn for the little pies, or we become friends with those we don't already know, or the occasional fight will break out.

There are patty shops of renown, such as Tastees. When I was a little girl, it was Bruce's, and then there is Angel Flake. You see, we regularly fall in love with one particular patty from one particular vendor, and it is like a love affair. We must have that patty, and only that patty. But if the recipe changes in the slightest, we fall out of love. There is very little that the patty shop owner can do to entice us back. We will immediately search for a new patty shop, and soon everyone is hearing praises about the new patty shop, and we have totally forgotten our previous allegiance.

Why is a patty so good? The crust, the crust, the crust! Patties are usually made with a beef filling, but there are also seafood patties, mainly lobster. These patties are available

Pastry

4 cups all-purpose flour
½ teaspoon baking powder
1 teaspoon ground
   turmeric
1 teaspoon salt
1 cup solid vegetable
   shortening, at room
   temperature
Approximately 1 cup very
   cold water

Filling

2 medium-sized onions
3 scallions, including tops
2 hot peppers, preferably
   Scotch bonnets
1½ pounds ground beef or
   chuck
2 tablespoons oil
5 cups fresh bread crumbs
   (¾ pound)
¾ teaspoon ground thyme
¾ teaspoon ground tur-
   meric
Salt and pepper to taste
¾ to 1 cup water

frozen in most West Indian stores, or they can be made fresh at home. They can be mild or hot and usually a vendor will ask which you prefer.

Then there are little cocktail patties—little bites that are served as appetizers. The patty purist will tell you that a patty can be eaten only freshly baked, but I find that they can be frozen and then rebaked very successfully.

To make the Pastry, sift together the flour, baking powder, turmeric, and salt. Cut in the shortening with a pastry blender or 2 knives until the dough has the consistency of cornmeal. Gradually add just enough cold water to hold the dough together, mixing it in with your fingers or a dough hook. The key, however, is never overwork your dough!

Wrap the dough in foil or plastic wrap and refrigerate while you prepare the Filling. You may also refrigerate the dough as long as overnight, but then you will need to give it 15 minutes to warm up before using.

To prepare the Filling, mince the onions, scallions, and peppers in a food processor, or chop very finely by hand. Add to the beef and mix well. Heat the oil in a Dutch oven or large skillet, then cook the meat mixture in it until just lightly browned, about 10 minutes. Add the bread crumbs and seasonings and stir well. Add the water. Cover and simmer for 20 to 30 minutes, as needed to evaporate excess liquid. The mixture should be just wet, not runny or dry. Allow to cool while you roll out the Pastry.

Preheat the oven to 400° F. Divide the dough into 24 even-sized pieces. On a lightly floured surface, roll out each piece of dough to a thickness of about $^3/_8$ inch—a little thicker than pie dough—and cut into a circle using a small saucer (approximately 4 inches across). Keep the patty dough circles moist by stacking and covering with a damp cloth. After all the circles are cut, take one at a time, and spoon on enough Filling to cover half of the circle. Fold the other half over, and seal the edges by crimping with a fork.

Bake the patties on ungreased baking sheets for 30 to 35 minutes. Serve hot when possible; however, Jamaicans will eat them any way they can!

YIELD: 24 PATTIES

"Wid It"

Festival
Bammy
Baked Sweet Potatoes
Baked Breadfruit
Fried Plantains
Baked Plantains
Jamaican Cole Slaw
Rice & Peas
Gungo Peas & Rice
Grilled Pineapple with
    Passion Fruit Butter
Steamed Callaloo
Honey-Ginger Dipping Sauce
Honey-Soy Dipping Sauce
Tamarind-Apricot Sauce
Fresh Mango Chutney with
    Banana & Jerk Seasoning

We buy our jerked foods from road stands—the pork is sold by the pound, the chicken is sold in quarters, and one says in a *very* loud voice: "Gimme ¼ chicken please and ½ pound pork."

These are usually served in pieces of aluminum foil with the juices dripping. If you are lucky there will be napkins available. The accompanying question usually is, "Wha' you have wid it?"

"Wha' you want? Me have festival, hard dough bread, roasted breadfruit, roasted yam, and sweet potatoes."

Many of these wonderful finger foods can be made at home so you can enjoy them with your jerked foods.

Festival is a relatively new food. It appeared on the Jamaican culinary scene only some ten years ago, but it is already a must. Eating a piece of festival is like eating a slightly sweet hush puppy without the onions, or a piece of fried corn bread that is much lighter and fluffier in texture. Hard dough bread is a little like eating a soft, chewy bagel. It is never baked at home. As for getting a recipe to pass on, it is impossible. The commercial makers tell me they do not have the recipe written down; they know it by heart—and keep it a secret.

Festival is featured on our Helshire beaches and at roadside stands. Helshire Beach is where all Kingstonians congregate, about 11 miles outside of Kingston at the foot of the South Helshire Hills. Laughter rings from the hills there, where Jamaican families of all classes come together. One sees fishermen going out and coming back in from the sea, mostly with dreadlocks or looking like Rastas.

We go there mainly for breakfast on a Saturday or a Sunday morning. Breakfast at Helshire consists of fried fish, bammy and festival, which is cooked fresh in little stands on the beach.

All fried fish in Jamaica is served with bammy, which is a very bland bread-like product. We eat it more for the texture than the flavor. Bammy is made of cassava, a starchy tuberous root, which is also known as yucca to those of Spanish heritage. For another frame of reference, it is the same plant that gives us tapioca, or the American Indians' manioc. There are two types of cassava: sweet and bitter. The sweet cassava is used to make bammy, whereas the bitter cassava makes a wonderful starch, which is used in abundance for all the children's clothes in Jamaica, where even the poorest child goes to school in clothes that are stiffly starched and ironed.

Bammies are like Jamaican beef patties in that they are very rarely made at home. The only recipe I have ever seen for bammies is one that came from Norma Benghiat. I have never made bammy myself, nor has my mother or grandmother or any of my aunts. We buy bammy from bammy women. When my father visits me from Jamaica, he brings up bammy, which I keep in the freezer. And if you go to Jamaica, I recommend you do the same, because, you see, making bammy is a lot of work.

To make bammy you have to peel and very finely grate some sweet cassava. You add about 1 teaspoon salt for every 4 cups of grated cassava and mix; this draws out the moisture in the cassava. Then you press out the excess liquid through a sieve. After that it's simply a matter of making bammy cakes about 6 inches in diameter and frying them for about 5 minutes on each side.

Before eating store-bought or homemade bammy you must soak each one in a shallow bowl filled with 1 cup milk that is mixed with a dash of salt for about 10 minutes. Then fry, grill, or bake them. I prefer to bake them for about 15 minutes in a 350° F. oven with a little butter on them.

Yams are large edible roots that should not be confused with sweet potatoes. Yams are usually white and come in a variety of shapes and sizes. My grandmother especially loved a variety called Yellow Yam that was the color of butter. She looked for yams that were very dry and waxy. Although not as common as sweet potatoes, yams can be found in the States, especially in produce markets that cater to a Hispanic clientele.

With jerk chicken or pork, yams are usually left in their skins and baked over the same coals as the meat. But yams can also be peeled and boiled in soups or served mashed. As far as cooking, treat yams as you would sweet potatoes and you can't go wrong.

Sweet potatoes are what Latins call *boniatos* or *batatas*. Eaten in large quantities by both Latins and Jamaicans, sweet potatoes are purplish brown to red in color, and slightly sweet in taste. They are almost powdery in texture after baking. In Jamaica, sweet potatoes are put to more varied uses than in the States and are found boiled and in soups and make the most wonderful desserts.

Breadfruit is a large, round, green, starchy vegetable grown from enormous, elegant plants. The fruit has a pebbled green skin. Inside, the meat is white. One breadfruit can feed a whole family—roasted, mashed, or boiled, just as you would a potato. The texture of breadfruit is lighter than that of a potato, however, more like bread.

Breadfruit is usually roasted over hot coals and served with jerk pork or chicken. You can also roast breadfruit in your oven. Because of its size, it will take around 2 hours to bake.

Most Jamaicans' favorite variety of breadfruit is called Yellow Heart. The flesh is slightly sweet and it tastes and looks just like butter. This variety is a little difficult to find, but if you get the opportunity, buy it! Roast breadfruit and pear (avocado) served together (sliced, not mashed) is a real treat in Jamaica. If you can make it with a Yellow Heart and Simmons (a variety of avocado), you have heaven!

You can find fresh breadfuit in Spanish and West Indian

markets. Treat it like a potato and store it in a cool, dry place. I do not peel breadfruit before baking it, but I do peel it for any other form of cooking.

A dish that must go in all Jamaican cookbooks is our Jamaican rice and peas (called peas and rice in the Bahamas). In Jamaica, we have two versions—one made with red kidney beans, which is served throughout the year, and the other made with fresh gungo (pronounced goongo) peas, served mainly at Christmastime.

These dishes also accompany jerk pork, chicken, or fish, but would be served in a restaurant or in the home, as it would be a little difficult to serve rice and peas in the standard foil of the jerk shacks!

Another side dish, or "wid it" dish, is plantain. Now let me tell you about plantain, which is the big sister to the banana. It may be up to 3 times bigger than the standard Cavendish banana that everyone knows how to use, thanks to large companies like Dole and Chiquita. The plantain, however, is still something of a mystery. One can buy it in most supermarkets or open air markets, but what to do with it after you have bought it? Let's address that question.

We in the islands cannot live without plantains. They are eaten at every stage of maturity from green to ripe. In Jamaica, green plantains are fried and eaten as chips. We eat "turn" (partially ripe) plantains boiled in soup. Ripe plantains, which are black in color and may look rotten to the uninformed, are either baked or fried and served as a side dish, or made into a dessert called plantain tarts. So you see, what would we do without plantains?

The green to yellow plantains that you will see in the supermarket are not fully ripe. No problem! Buy them as they are, take them home, and wrap them in newspaper for 4 to 5

days, by which time they should be much softer. Never ever put them in the refrigerator, as this will alter their flavor. With this little message I hope that the next time you encounter a plantain in your local market, you will pick it up and take it with you. Bake or fry it; that is island eating!

Festival

1 cup all-purpose flour
1 cup cornmeal
2 teaspoons sugar
Pinch salt
¼ teaspoon ground nutmeg
¼ teaspoon baking soda
½ teaspoon vanilla extract
Approximately ½ cup milk
Oil for deep-frying

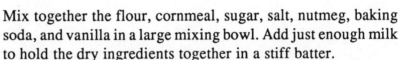

A must with any jerk dish, festival is a sweetened cousin to hush puppies. Allow about 2 pieces of festival per serving.

Mix together the flour, cornmeal, sugar, salt, nutmeg, baking soda, and vanilla in a large mixing bowl. Add just enough milk to hold the dry ingredients together in a stiff batter.

Preheat the oil in either a deep-fat fryer or in a skillet—the oil must be deep enough to completely cover the Festival. Heat the oil to about 370° F. If, when you add a piece of dough, the Festival begins to brown immediately, the oil is too hot!

Pinch off pieces of dough and form into cylinders that are approximately 4 inches long and 1½ inches in diameter. Fry a few at a time until golden brown; be sure that the inside is cooked. Drain well. Serve with jerk pork or fried fish and bammy.

YIELD: 6 TO 7 SERVINGS

Baked Sweet Potatoes

4 medium-sized sweet
  potatoes
4 teaspoons vegetable oil
Butter (optional)

In the jerk shacks, sweet potatoes are just put on the coals and baked for about an hour. The aroma of browning potatoes is wonderful as it mingles with the jerk products. At home, I like to bake my sweet potatoes in the oven.

Preheat the oven to 350° F. Wash the potatoes well and dry. Rub the skin of each potato with oil. Bake for 1 hour, or until soft when pierced with a knife.

Split each potato down the middle and drizzle with butter if you like. Serve with jerk chicken. You are in for a treat!

YIELD: 4 SERVINGS

Baked Breadfruit

1 medium-sized bread-
   fruit, 2 to 3 pounds
4 teaspoons vegetable oil

Jamaica experienced one of the worst hurricanes in history during September 1988. Gilbert devastated everything in its path, including a lot of wonderful breadfruit trees. We really miss them and eagerly await the growth of the new crop.

Preheat the oven to 350° F. Rub the skin of the breadfruit with oil. Bake for 1½ to 2 hours, depending on the size of the breadfruit. The breadfruit will have a pleasant aroma when it is done, and will yield to the pressure if you press it with your finger, as a baked potato would. Peel and wrap in a damp cloth until you are ready to serve (you can hold it for several hours before serving). Slice thinly and serve.

The next day, if any breadfruit is left, it is delicious deep-fried for chips. These make a wonderful accompaniment for cold drinks.

YIELD: 6 SERVINGS

Fried Plantains

2 pounds ripe (black)
  plantains
¼ cup vegetable oil
1 tablespoon butter
  (optional, but I find that
  it makes the plantain
  taste even more
  delicious)

Fried plantains accompany almost every meal in Jamaica.

Cut each plantain lengthwise into 4 thick strips; then peel; or cut into quarters, then peel and cut on the diagonal to make 1-inch rounds. In a very heavy skillet, heat the oil and then add the butter. Add some plantain slices. (Be careful not to add too many slices at the same time, as this will lower the temperature of the oil.) Fry for about 1½ minutes per side, or until golden brown, turning once. As they brown, transfer the pieces to paper towels to absorb whatever trace of oil they may have retained. Serve hot.

YIELD: 4 TO 6 SERVINGS

Baked Plantains

2 yellow plantains with black flecks

Baked plantains are a good alternative when you are trying to avoid fried foods. Use partially ripe plantains for this dish.

Preheat the oven to 350° F. Oil a baking sheet.

Peel the plantains, leaving one strip of skin. Cut the plantains in thirds crosswise. Place them skin side down on the baking sheet. Bake for 35 to 40 minutes, or until soft. Cool, completely peel the skin, and slice the plantain lengthwise. These can be served warm or at room temperature.

YIELD: 6 SERVINGS

Rice & Peas

1½ cups dried red kidney
 beans or 1 (16-ounce)
 can cooked kidney beans
 (see note below)
1 garlic clove, crushed
4 cups water (3 cups if
 using canned beans)
Salt
2 strips of bacon, chopped
2 cups coconut milk
Freshly ground pepper
1 scallion, chopped
1 sprig fresh thyme
1 whole fresh Scotch
 bonnet hot pepper
2 cups uncooked white rice

Jamaican rice and peas is a staple of our diet, and we use coconut milk in it to give it a characteristically sweet flavor.

Rice and peas can be cooked 7 days a week. My cousins, Michael and Richard, now grown men, were voracious eaters as teenagers. For their Sunday evening supper, they were known to make a rice and peas and plantain sandwich that consisted of an entire loaf of sliced bread—yes, about 20 slices—and in between each slice were packed rice and peas, gravy, and fried plantains. Both boys grew to be well over 6 feet tall and one is now a professor of English at the University of Massachusetts. But pity my poor Aunt Vie, who always thought she had made enough food to last for 2 more days with her Sunday rice and peas . . .

All recipes for rice and peas are more or less the same. This one I've adapted from *Island Cooking* by Dunstan Harris (The Crossing Press).

Combine the kidney beans, garlic, water, and salt to taste in a saucepan. Cook, covered, over medium heat until tender, about 2 hours. Add the coconut milk, freshly ground pepper to taste, scallion, thyme, and fresh whole pepper. (Be careful to keep the pepper intact; we want the flavor and aroma from the pepper, not the heat.) Then add the rice and stir. Return to a boil. Then cover, reduce the heat, and simmer for about 25 minutes, or until the liquids have been absorbed. Serve hot as a side dish.

Rice & Peas continued . . .

Note: If dried beans are not available, 1 (16-ounce) can of red kidney beans can be substituted. Drain and combine with 3 cups water and the other ingredients except the rice and bacon. Bring to a boil, reduce the heat, and simmer for 5 minutes. Add the rice and bacon and stir with a fork. Bring to a boil, reduce the heat, and cook for about 20 minutes, or until all the liquids are absorbed.

YIELD: 6 SERVINGS

Gungo Peas & Rice

¼ pound bacon, diced
1 scallion, diced
1 garlic clove, crushed
1 sprig fresh thyme or 1½ teaspoons dried thyme
1 cup fresh gungo peas or 1 (16-ounce) can pigeon peas
4 cups water (3 cups if using canned peas)
Salt and freshly ground pepper
2 cups uncooked white rice

Gungo (pronounced goongo) peas and rice is a delicacy at home. It was my mother's favorite dish, especially for Christmas. We would plant our peas during the month of September, as most Jamaicans do, to reap for Christmas. Gungo peas take about 8 weeks to bear and have a wonderful fresh green color. On the other islands, they are known as pigeon peas and are dried, but we like them fresh. If you cannot grow them in your locale, gungo peas are available in most markets, usually dried or canned.

Fry the bacon in a large Dutch oven until the fat has been released. Add the scallion and garlic and sauté until translucent. Add the thyme, fresh peas, and water. Cook until tender—1 to 2 hours, adding more water if needed. If you are using canned pigeon peas, cook for only 5 to 10 minutes. Add salt and pepper to taste.

Add the rice, bring to a boil, and stir. Reduce the heat and simmer, covered, for about 20 minutes, or until the liquid is absorbed. Serve hot as a side dish.

YIELD: 6 SERVINGS

Jamaican Cole Slaw

4 cups shredded cabbage
¾ cup shredded carrots
½ cup chopped nuts
   (I like walnuts)
½ cup mayonnaise
2 tablespoons sugar
1 tablespoon cider vinegar
2 tablespoons Dry Jerk
   Seasoning (page 16)

I prefer green cabbage in my cole slaw. You may add a little red cabbage to give it color.

Combine the cabbage, carrots, and nuts in a large bowl; set aside. Mix together the mayonnaise, sugar, vinegar, and seasoning. Spoon over the cabbage mixture. Toss well. Cover and chill before serving.

YIELD: 4 TO 6 SERVINGS

Grilled Pineapple with Passion Fruit Butter

1 pineapple, with green
   leaves still
   attached
3 tablespoons butter,
   melted
3 tablespoons Passion
   Fruit Sauce (page 146)
2 tablespoons toasted
   chopped cashews

Heat up your grill for delicious jerk chicken or pork and then cook this delightful pineapple dish as an accompaniment.

Stoke up your grill if it is not already hot. Quarter the pineapple lengthwise, leaving the green leaves on. Mix the melted butter and Passion Fruit Sauce. Grill the pineapple on one side until golden, approximately 5 minutes. Turn the fruit and brush the cooked side with the passion fruit-butter sauce. Cook the other side for 5 minutes, then brush with more of the sauce mixture.

To serve, place the pineapple quarters on an attractive platter and pour the remaining sauce over top. Garnish with the cashews. As an alternative to the cashews, try toasted coconut flakes. Each person should take a quarter and slice the fruit away from the skin. Delicious!

YIELD: 4 SERVINGS

Steamed Callaloo

6 pounds callaloo, chopped
2 tablespoons butter
3 onions, peeled and diced
2 tablespoons Dry Jerk
   Seasoning (page 16)
1 cup water
1 small (8-ounce) can
   tomato sauce

Callaloo is a big, leafy green that is commonly available in Jamaica. If you are very lucky, a friend will bring it to you in big bunches when they come in from the country. Callaloo can often be found in West Indian groceries; if you can't locate any, you can substitute mustard greens or spinach, but it won't be the same.

This recipe comes from my friend Eli Rickham.

Wash the callaloo in lots of water, discarding the old outer leaves. Make sure that the stalks are cut into small pieces. The stalks of the callaloo should be easily pierced. If they are too old, they will be pithy inside and have a bitter taste.

In a large pot, melt the butter. Add the onions and sauté until almost translucent. Add the Dry Jerk Seasoning, water, and tomato sauce. Add the chopped callaloo. Cover and simmer over medium to low heat for 15 to 20 minutes. Adjust the seasonings to taste. I never use much salt. Serve hot.

YIELD: 6 SERVINGS

Honey-Ginger Dipping Sauce

1 (8-ounce) can sweetened
  tamarind nectar
1 tablespoon honey
1 thumb (2 to 3 inches)
  fresh ginger root, grated
1 tablespoon soy sauce
1 tablespoon Dry Jerk
  Seasoning (page 16)
1 teaspoon cornstarch
1 teaspoon water

This dipping sauce is delicious with all jerked meats and fish. Most of the sweetness is derived from the tamarind nectar. Cans of the nectar can be found in West Indian specialty food stores or in Oriental food stores.

Combine the tamarind nectar with the honey and boil until it is reduced by one third of its volume. Stir in the ginger, soy sauce, and Dry Jerk Seasoning. Mix the cornstarch with the water to form a paste, and then mix with the tamarind mixture. Continue to cook and stir continuously, until the sauce thickens. Serve hot or cold.

YIELD: APPROXIMATELY 1¼ CUPS

Honey-Soy Dipping Sauce

3 tablespoons soy sauce
3 tablespoons honey
2 tablespoons red wine
   vinegar
1 teaspoon Dry Jerk
   Seasoning (page 16)
1½ teaspoons cornstarch
¼ cup water

This makes a great glaze for chicken legs and pork loin. Its flavor is not unlike Chinese hoisin sauce.

Mix the soy sauce, honey, vinegar, and jerk seasoning in a saucepan and bring to a boil. Mix together the cornstarch and the water. Stir into the sauce and cook until thickened. Serve hot or cold.

YIELD: ¾ CUP

Tamarind-Apricot Sauce

1 (8-ounce) can sweetened
   tamarind nectar
4 ounces apricot jam
2 tablespoons honey
1 teaspoon Dijon-style
   mustard (optional)

This can be served as a condiment with meats. The sauce is also used to prepare Medallions of Pork (page 36).

Combine the tamarind nectar and apricot jam and bring to a boil. Continue to boil until the mixture thickens. Stir in the honey. Add the mustard if desired. Serve cold.

YIELD: APPROXIMATELY 1½ CUPS

Fresh Mango Chutney with Banana & Jerk Seasoning

¼ cup golden raisins
¼ cup water
½ cup firmly packed
   brown sugar
½ cup chopped onion
¾ cup cider vinegar
1 tablespoon Dry Jerk
   Seasoning (page 16)
Juice and rind of 1 lime
   or lemon
1½ cups peeled diced
   mango (mango should be
   underripe, not yellow)
2 teaspoons hot pepper
   sauce
1 tablespoon Pickapeppa
   Sauce (see page 19)
1 teaspoon peeled minced
   ginger root
1 ripe banana, diced

This chutney is delicious as a condiment with pork, chicken, fish, or shrimp.

Soak the raisins in hot water to plump for about 30 minutes.

In a nonaluminum saucepan, bring the ¼ cup water, sugar, onion, and vinegar to a boil. Add the Dry Jerk Seasoning, lime juice and rind, diced mango, hot sauce, Pickapeppa Sauce, and ginger. Reduce the heat and simmer uncovered for 30 minutes, or until the mixture becomes thick. Stir in the plumped raisins and banana. Cover and chill before serving; this will keep for at least 2 weeks in the refrigerator.

YIELD: APPROXIMATELY 4 CUPS

Tropical Sweet Tooth

Jamaican Fruit Salad

Baked Bananas with Tamarind Sauce

Tropical Trifle

Key Lime Pie

White Chocolate Passion

Coffee Ice Cream Bombe

Coffee Mousse

Cold Coffee Soufflé

Bread Pudding

Cornmeal Pone

Plantain Tarts

Gizadas

Totoes

Banana Bread

Honey Pineapple Bread

Quick Orange Bread

Rum Custard

Passion Fruit Sauce

9-Inch Pie Crust

Jamaicans have a real sweet tooth—and is it any wonder, with so much tropical fruit there for our enjoyment? Our most popular dessert is a fruit salad, which we make with whatever is in season—mangoes, bananas, pineapples, oranges, and papayas. This fruit salad is usually made up about once a day and kept in the refrigerator for snacking on all day long.

Then we have heavier fare designed to fill the belly, reflecting the era of the plantation days, when slaves would make cornmeal pone, sweet potato puddings, and totoes. And what is a toto, you ask? It is a soft, sweet biscuit that makes a wonderful snack.

But that doesn't begin to explain the appeal of totoes to a Jamaican. Picture this. It is lunch break at school and the students tumble out of the classrooms by the hundreds. The street vendors are poised and ready to make their sales to the youngsters. They have glass and wooden cases, which they unloaded from buses and cars, along with the baskets they carried on their heads. In the cases are the Jamaican delights that are as basic to Jamaica as jerk chicken—totoes, gizadas, sweet potato pudding, *bullas*, plantain tarts, bustamante back-bone, and paradise plum. Instead of buying a balanced lunch as instructed by their mothers, the children descend upon the vendors with an appetite for pure sweets.

Some of these sweets you can make for yourself in your own homes; others you must come to Jamaica to try. The names may be unfamiliar, but the sweets are not terribly exotic. A gizada, for instance, is a coconut tartlet—delicious and chewy. A *bulla* is a wonderful sweet made of water, sugar, and flour—it fills the belly. Paradise plums are red and yellow hard rock candies, colored to look like our native plums. Bustamante backbone is a very sweet coconut confection that takes quite a bit of work to make; we don't see it as much as we used to.

(Bustamante was a popular prime minister back in the fifties, and I believe this sweet was named for him.) In this chapter you will find recipes for totoes, gizadas, and plantain tarts, as well as fancier desserts.

You see, in the hotels, one finds gourmet desserts all based on tropical fruits but done in the European manner, such as guava tarts and trifles. Some of these desserts are as easy to make as combining slices of mango with vanilla ice cream. Topped with a rum-flavored custard, you have heaven!

None of these desserts are served at jerk shacks, but they certainly are featured in every Jamaican household on a Sunday and at buffets where jerk is one of the featured highlights—and in every school cafeteria and at many roadside stands.

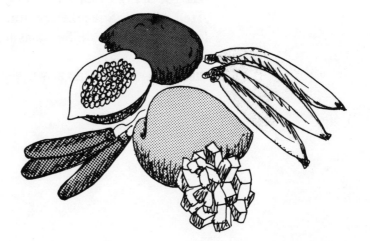

Jamaican Fruit Salad

1 mango
2 oranges
1 papaya (small or
   medium)
1 banana (optional)
Juice of 1 lime or lemon
½ pineapple (or 2 cups
   canned pineapple
   chunks if fresh pine-
   apple is not available)

In a lot of homes, this salad is made on a daily basis. Instead of having a cookie for a snack, we eat fruit salad.

One uses the fruits that are in season—if the fruit salad is to sit all day in the refrigerator to furnish an ongoing snack, I omit the bananas because they turn dark if left exposed for an extended period of time. If the salad is to be used on a buffet or eaten immediately, then I include the bananas.

Fruit salad is not usually made on a per serving basis since it is expected to keep in the refrigerator. Usually it is designed to fill a medium-sized bowl, as it is here.

Peel the skin from all the fruits. Remove the seeds from the mango, oranges, and the papaya. Cut all the fruits into bite-sized pieces. Squeeze the lime over all the fruits and mix together. Chill well. Serve as is, or with vanilla ice cream.

YIELD: 1 MEDIUM-SIZED BOWL

Baked Bananas with Tamarind Sauce

4 ripe bananas
¼ cup Tamarind-Apricot Sauce (page 120)
¼ cup packaged sweetened flaked coconut
¼ cup slivered almonds
1 tablespoon brown sugar
2 tablespoons melted butter (do not substitute margarine!)
Juice of 1 lime or lemon

This dish can be served as a side dish to accompany meats or as a dessert, by itself or with ice cream.

Preheat the oven to 350° F. Peel the bananas and split lengthwise. Arrange in a buttered, shallow casserole dish. Spoon the tamarind sauce over the bananas, then top with the coconut and almonds. Mix the brown sugar with the melted butter and pour over the bananas. Bake ripe bananas for 20 minutes; if the bananas are not very ripe, bake for 30 minutes. Serve hot.

YIELD: 4 SERVINGS

Tropical Trifle

3 (12-ounce) cans
   evaporated milk
4 cups whole milk
1 cup sugar
6 egg yolks, lightly beaten
2 tablespoons dessert
   (sweet) sherry
1 teaspoon vanilla extract
1 cup sliced strawberries
2 tablespoons sugar
Approximately 12 slices
   day-old pound cake or
   24 lady fingers or 36
   macaroons
2 or 3 mangoes, peeled and
   sliced
4 or 5 kiwi fruit, peeled
   and sliced
1 cup seedless grapes,
   preferably red, sliced in
   half

In the early 1970s, my husband and I catered a private dinner party and then a large reception in honor of a visit by Queen Elizabeth. How proud I was as I prepared the dinner for one hundred of Jamaica's finest citizens and the royal party. I was determined to serve the best and sweetest mangoes in a variation of trifle that I felt sure would impress the Queen and her entire party. Only I did not plan on the electricity going out that very day. What a mess! Luckily I had friends at the Kingshouse facilities (which had a battery-powered generator) and they came through for me to finish the trifle of trifles. (Yes, it was a smashing success.)

The classic dish to prepare this in is a clear, footed, round dish with sides approximately 7 to 8 inches tall.

Heat both milks in a saucepan over low heat, and then add the 1 cup sugar and egg yolks. Continue to cook, stirring constantly, until the mixture becomes very thick. Do not allow to boil, as this will cause curdling. Add the sherry and vanilla. Remove from the heat and allow to cool.

Combine the strawberries with the 2 tablespoons sugar and set aside.

Line a trifle dish (or any clear, deep dish) with slices of cake or lady fingers or macaroons. (Slices of cake should be about 1 inch thick, ladyfingers should be halved, and macaroons left whole.) Pour half the cooled custard over the cake, then add half the fruit. Add another layer of cake and top with the

remaining custard, then fruit. Refrigerate until you are ready to serve.

If you are serving to adults only, you may want to sprinkle a little extra sherry over the cake. I love trifle this way, but trifle is always so popular with children that I seldom get to serve it with the extra sherry.

YIELD: 8 TO 10 SERVINGS

Key Lime Pie

Pie
4 egg yolks
1 egg white
1 (14-ounce) can
   sweetened condensed
   milk
½ cup freshly squeezed
   lime juice
¼ teaspoon salt
9-Inch Pie Crust (page
   147), baked, then chilled

Meringue
3 egg whites
½ teaspoon cream of tartar
6 tablespoons sugar

Although the lime is very important to Jamaica, almost more basic to our cuisine is the condensed milk also found in the recipe. All Jamaicans use condensed milk. Not only is canned milk more reliable in a land with unreliable electricity, it is considered a great delicacy. Jamaicans use the sweetened variety in their coffee, so do not offer a Jamaican plain cream and sugar, but rather the wonderful canned nectar. It is also mixed with stout, and in other drinks, such as papaya juice and soursop. Children who do not want to take their medicine find it a little more palatable to swallow it when mixed with condensed milk.

Our local limes resemble the very tart, wild key lime found in the Florida Keys. However, it is very difficult to find these off the island, so this recipe uses the more common Persian lime, readily available in U.S. markets.

Beat the egg yolks and the 1 egg white until they are very thick and lemon-colored. Add the condensed milk, lime juice, and salt. Do not beat, but stir until well blended. Pour into the baked and chilled pie shell. Refrigerate for several hours to allow the filling to gel.

Preheat the oven to 425° F.

Shortly before serving time, beat the 3 egg whites with the cream of tartar until they form rounded peaks. Gradually beat in the sugar, and continue beating until it is dissolved. By then the Meringue should be stiff and glossy. Spread over the filling, being sure to seal the edges well so that the Meringue will not shrink.

Bake for 5 to 7 minutes, or until the Meringue is delicately browned. Cool away from drafts. This is delicious with a cup of Blue Mountain coffee for dessert.

YIELD: 6 SERVINGS

White Chocolate Passion

4 ounces white chocolate
¼ cup Passion Fruit Sauce
  (page 146)
¼ cup water
3 dozen juicy ripe
  strawberries or fruit of
  your choice

This delicious fondue treat of white chocolate and passion fruit is beautiful and adapts well to entertaining large or small groups. Surround the bowl of warm sauce with attractively arranged fruits. This is particularly good with strawberries, mangoes, pears, and apples.

Melt the white chocolate over a double boiler or in the microwave. (To melt in the microwave, cook at very low heat, at not more than 30 percent power. Stir often.)

Mix the Passion Fruit Sauce with the water; then add the passion fruit mix to the melted white chocolate. Stir until well mixed and smooth.

To serve, place the chocolate mixture in an attractive bowl surrounded by fruit on a platter. Don't forget the hors d'oeuvre picks (or toothpicks)!

YIELD: 9 TO 10 SERVINGS

Coffee Ice Cream Bombe

1 quart coffee ice cream
1 pint French vanilla ice
  cream
½ cup chopped toasted
  cashews
Whipped cream
Coffee bean candies or
  nuts (optional garnish)
Tia Maria or any
  coffee-flavored liqueur

Place a 1½-quart metal mixing bowl or bombe mold in the freezer overnight.

Set aside 1 cup of coffee ice cream for the top of the bombe, then soften the rest of the coffee ice cream. Use a large spoon to spread the ice cream in the bowl around the bottom and up the sides. Return the container to the freezer to chill until firm.

In a medium-sized bowl, mix the vanilla ice cream and chopped nuts. Pack the ice cream mix into the middle of the coffee ice cream bowl. Stop about 1 inch short of the top.

Soften the remaining coffee ice cream and use it to fill the bowl the rest of the way. Cover well and place the bombe in the freezer until you are ready to serve.

To serve, remove the bombe from the freezer and invert onto a serving platter. Wet a dish towel, wrap it around the mold, and hold it there for a few minutes. This should allow you to remove the mold easily from the bombe. Decorate with whipped cream and coffee bean candies or nuts if desired. Drizzle Tia Maria over the slices as they are served.

YIELD: 10 SERVINGS

Coffee Mousse

½ cup whipping cream
¾ cup sugar
½ cup warm water
1 tablespoon unflavored gelatin
2 tablespoons instant coffee powder, preferably espresso
4 egg whites
¼ cup finely grated semisweet chocolate

This delicious Coffee Mousse will make you believe you are having dessert on the veranda of a luxurious estate in Jamaica. Serve with coconut biscuits, either homemade or purchased.

Beat the cream with ¼ cup of the sugar until soft peaks form. Set aside.

Pour the warm water into a small bowl. Sprinkle the gelatin over the water and stir well to dissolve. Add the coffee and stir well until dissolved. Fold into the whipped cream. Beat the egg whites until soft peaks form, then add the remaining ½ cup sugar. Beat constantly until very stiff.

Fold the beaten whites into the whipped cream. Fold in the grated chocolate. Chill until you are ready to serve. Serve in your prettiest footed dessert bowls or parfait glasses.

YIELD: 6 SERVINGS

Cold Coffee Soufflé

1½ cups cold brewed
coffee
⅔ cup sugar
1 tablespoon unflavored
gelatin
½ cup milk
3 eggs, separated
¼ teaspoon salt
1 teaspoon vanilla extract
Whipped cream
Coffee bean candies
(optional garnish)

This makes a delightful centerpiece for a dessert table. I use my fanciest mold and find it very helpful to grease the mold with a spray oil.

Combine the coffee, ⅓ cup of the sugar, the gelatin, and milk in a saucepan. Heat over low heat or in the microwave until the gelatin is dissolved. Slightly beat the egg yolks and add along with the remaining ⅓ cup sugar and salt.

Continue to cook over low heat or in the microwave until the mixture thickens slightly. Remove the mixture from the heat and add the vanilla. Cool, stirring often. As your soufflé begins to gel, slightly beat the egg whites and fold in. Pour into a decorative mold and chill.

To serve, turn out onto a platter and garnish with whipped cream and coffee bean candies if desired.

YIELD: 6 TO 8 SERVINGS

Bread Pudding

**1 pound day-old white
  sandwich bread or rolls,
  crusts removed**
½ cup sugar
**¾ teaspoon ground
  cinnamon**
¼ teaspoon ground nutmeg
¼ cup light or dark rum
½ cup raisins
¼ cup melted butter
**½ cup sweetened
  condensed milk**
4 cups whole milk
5 eggs, well beaten

This Bread Pudding is a favorite of my father. It will rise beautifully in the oven, turn a wonderful golden brown, and yield a creamy consistency. The condensed milk gives it a rich, smooth taste, just barely flavored with the rum.

Preheat the oven to 350° F. Grease an 8-inch or 9-inch square baking dish.

Break up the bread into small cubes. Mix together the bread, sugar, cinnamon, nutmeg, rum, raisins, and melted butter in a large mixing bowl. Pour into the baking dish.

Combine the condensed milk, whole milk, and eggs and pour over the bread mixture. (If you are using an 8-inch dish, place it on a baking sheet to avoid spills.) Bake for 1 to 1¼ hours, or until a knife inserted in the middle comes out clean. Serve warm or cooled. This is delicious with ice cream, whipped cream, Rum Custard (page 145), or hard sauce.

YIELD: 6 TO 8 SERVINGS

Cornmeal Pone

Cornmeal Pone
2¾ cups cornmeal
⅓ cup all-purpose flour
6 cups coconut milk
2⅔ cups firmly packed
   brown sugar
½ teaspoon ground nutmeg
1 tablespoon vanilla
   extract
¼ cup light or dark rum
1⅓ cups raisins

Topping
1 cup coconut milk
½ cup firmly packed
   brown sugar
¼ cup butter

My friend Norma Benghiat, with whom I went to school, is one of Jamaica's leading food researchers. She is the author of several articles and cookbooks. This is her version of the rich, dense Jamaican cornmeal pone, and it is not at all similar to the corn pone made by the early settlers in the American colonies. Their corn pone was a plain corn cake baked in the oven. As you will see, the Jamaican cornmeal pone is a delightful pudding.

Preheat the oven to 300° F. Grease a 9-inch by 13-inch baking dish.

Combine the cornmeal and flour in a bowl. Add the coconut milk, a little at a time, mixing well until you have a smooth batter. Then stir in the rest of the Cornmeal Pone ingredients. The mixture should be liquid rather than thick. Pour it into the baking dish and bake for at least 1 hour, or until the pudding is set like a baked custard. Remove from the oven and cool until slightly firm. While the pone is still warm, mix together the Topping ingredients and pour over the pone. Bake for another 30 minutes, or until a toothpick inserted into the pone comes out clean.

Cool before cutting into squares and serving. Your family will enjoy Cornmeal Pone as either a dessert or a snack.

YIELD: 8 SERVINGS

Plantain Tarts

3 very ripe, black
  plantains
½ cup sugar
¼ to ½ teaspoon nutmeg
¼ teaspoon vanilla extract
  or to taste
Red food coloring
  (optional)
Sugar for garnish
Double recipe 9-Inch Pie
  Crust dough (page 147)

These tarts and the Gizadas that follow are favorites of Jamaican school children.

Peel the plantains. Boil in water to cover until tender, about 15 minutes. Drain and mash until they are smooth. Add the ½ cup sugar, nutmeg, vanilla, and a drop or two of red food coloring.

Preheat the oven to 400° F. Prepare the pie crust dough according to the recipe directions. Roll out the pastry and use a saucer or small plate to cut out 8 circles, each 4 to 5 inches in diameter.

Divide the plantain mix into 8 portions and place 1 portion on half of each of the pie dough circles. Fold the other half over to form a half circle, then crimp the edges with a fork. Sprinkle with sugar as a garnish.

Bake on ungreased baking sheets in the preheated oven for 30 to 45 minutes. Remove from the baking sheets and cool on wire racks. Serve hot or cool.

YIELD: 8 TARTS

Gizadas

1 ripe coconut, grated,
  or 1 (7-ounce) bag
  sweetened grated dry
  or frozen coconut
⅔ cup firmly packed
  brown sugar
½ teaspoon grated
  nutmeg
9-Inch Pie Crust dough
  (page 147)

Gizadas, oh gizadas—do they bring back memories from my childhood! As I have told you, every child in Jamaica buys from the sweets maker, and the gizada is high on the list of favorite treats! The coconut filling becomes almost chewy when cooked like this.

If you can't find a ripe coconut, and have a choice between dry or frozen coconut, choose the frozen. It is closer in taste and texture to fresh coconut.

Preheat the oven to 375° F. Lightly grease 2 baking sheets.

Mix together the coconut, brown sugar, and nutmeg thoroughly. Set aside.

Prepare the pie crust dough according to the recipe directions. Divide the dough into 4 equal portions. On a lightly floured surface, roll out the dough and cut into 1½-inch circles. Place a small amount of the coconut mixture on each dough circle. Fold up a small rim around the coconut filling to make a bowl. Place on the baking sheets and bake until browned, approximately 20 minutes. Remove to wire racks to cool. These are best served warm.

YIELD: ABOUT 4 DOZEN

Totoes

2 cups all-purpose flour
2 teaspoons baking
    powder
1 teaspoon ground
    cinnamon
½ teaspoon ground nutmeg
¼ cup butter or margarine
½ cup white sugar
½ cup firmly packed
    brown sugar
1 egg, beaten
2 teaspoons vanilla extract
Approximately ½ cup milk

A favorite with children, and nothing exotic is called for in this easily made snack. You should have all the ingredients on hand.

Preheat the oven to 375° F. Grease an 8-inch square pan.

Mix together the flour, baking powder, cinnamon, and nutmeg. Cream the butter and sugars until light; gradually add the flour mixture. Add the beaten egg, vanilla, and just enough milk to make the mixture into a stiff batter the consistency of cookie dough.

Spread the batter in the prepared pan. Bake for 30 to 35 minutes. Cool and cut into squares. If you have any leftovers, they will store well in an airtight container.

YIELD: 9 SERVINGS

Banana Bread

Bread

1 cup mashed ripe
   bananas
1 teaspoon lemon juice
½ cup solid vegetable
   shortening
1 cup white sugar
2 eggs
2 cups all-purpose flour
1 tablespoon baking
   powder
½ teaspoon salt
1 cup chopped nuts
   (optional)

Glaze

2 teaspoons brown sugar
¼ teaspoon ground
   cinnamon

This recipe makes a 1-pound loaf. I usually double the recipe and freeze the second loaf. This is delicious at teatime!

Preheat the oven to 350° F. Grease a 9-inch by 5-inch loaf pan.

As soon as you mash the bananas, combine with the lemon juice to prevent browning. Cream the shortening with the white sugar. Then add the eggs and cream well. Mix in the mashed bananas.

Sift together the flour, baking powder, and salt. Mix quickly into the banana mixture. Add the nuts if desired.

Pour the mixture into the loaf pan and bake for approximately 1¼ hours, or until a cake tester inserted in the center comes out clean. As soon as you take the banana bread from the oven, sprinkle with the brown sugar mixed with the cinnamon to make a beautiful glaze. Cool for approximately 10 minutes on a wire rack, and then remove from the pan. Continue to cool on a wire rack.

YIELD: 10 TO 12 SERVINGS

Honey Pineapple Bread

2 tablespoons vegetable oil
1 cup honey
1 egg
2¼ cups sifted all-purpose
  flour
1 tablespoon baking
  powder
½ teaspoon salt
¾ cup chopped roasted
  nuts
1 cup raw wheat bran
1 cup canned pineapple
  juice

Not only does the bran in this recipe add delicious texture to the bread, it also adds healthy fiber to your diet.

Preheat the oven to 350° F. Grease a 9-inch by 5-inch loaf pan.

Blend the oil and honey, then add the egg and mix well. Sift together the flour, baking powder, and salt. Mix ½ cup of the flour mixture with the nuts. Add about half the remaining flour mixture to the egg mixture and mix well. Mix in the bran and pineapple juice, then add the remaining flour mixture and nut mixture.

Pour into the loaf pan and bake for 1¼ hours, or until a cake tester inserted in the center comes out clean. Cool in the pan for approximately 10 minutes on a wire rack, and then remove from the pan. Continue to cool on a wire rack.

YIELD: 10 TO 12 SERVINGS

Quick Orange Bread

2 cups all-purpose flour
4 teaspoons baking
  powder
½ cup sugar
½ teaspoon salt
2 eggs
½ cup orange juice
3 tablespoons melted
  shortening or vegetable
  oil
½ cup chopped candied
  orange peel
½ teaspoon grated orange
  zest

Because of our British heritage, Jamaicans still enjoy after-noon tea. Usually we will serve toast with guava jelly and a piece of this type of sweet, cake-like bread. By the way, a cup of coffee is equally acceptable at teatime!

Preheat the oven to 350° F. Grease a 9-inch by 5-inch loaf pan.

Sift together the flour, baking powder, sugar, and salt. Beat the eggs well and add the orange juice, shortening, orange peel, and orange zest. Combine the egg mixture with the dry ingredients, mixing only enough to dampen all the flour.

Pour into the loaf pan and bake for 1 hour, or until a cake tester inserted in the center comes out clean. Cool in the pan for approximately 10 minutes on a wire rack, and then remove from pan. Continue to cool on a wire rack.

YIELD: 10 TO 12 SERVINGS

Rum Custard

1½ cups milk
¼ cup firmly packed light
   brown sugar
⅛ teaspoon salt
3 egg yolks, slightly beaten
2 tablespoons dark rum

This wonderful custard is delicious. Serve it over fresh fruits, such as mango, pineapple, papaya, or banana. You may also want to try it over cake or ice cream.

Combine the milk, brown sugar, and salt in the top of a double boiler. Heat slowly until bubbles appear and the sugar melts.

Mix a small part of the warm milk mixture into the beaten egg yolks and then return all of it to the top of the double boiler. Cook over simmering water for approximately 20 minutes, stirring constantly. Do not allow it to boil! Your custard is done when it will coat a clean metal spoon.

Cool slightly, then stir in the rum. Cover and cool to room temperature, then chill thoroughly before serving.

YIELD: APPROXIMATELY 2 CUPS (4 TO 5 SERVINGS)

Passion Fruit Sauce

2 passion fruits
1 cup sugar
1 cup water

If this seems too complicated for you, there is a commercially prepared passion fruit sauce available in the American market. Passion fruit is similar to tamarind in its extreme acidity. You will certainly want to dilute the pulp before tasting.

This sauce is very versatile and keeps for up to 2 weeks in the refrigerator if the container is kept tightly closed. I use the sauce in a few of the recipes in this chapter; it is also delicious over fresh fruit, or as a base for a seafood sauce.

Halve the passion fruits, and then scoop out the pulp and seeds. Discard the skin. Combine the fruit, sugar, and water in a saucepan and bring to a boil; then reduce the heat to a simmer. Cook until the pulp is soft, about 15 minutes. Press through a sieve, and then discard the pulp. When the fruit sauce is cool, store in the refrigerator in a tightly covered container.

YIELD: APPROXIMATELY 1½ CUPS

9-Inch Pie Crust

1 cup all-purpose flour
½ teaspoon salt
⅓ cup solid vegetable
   shortening
3 tablespoons ice water

My mother never cooked—but she sure knew how to make a good pie crust.

Sift together the flour and salt. Cut the shortening into the flour mixture with a pastry blender or 2 knives. Keep cutting until the particles are about the size of dried peas.

Add the water gradually, a few drops at a time, tossing the dough lightly with a fork to be sure that the water is distributed evenly. Gather the dough together to form a ball. Handle the dough as little as possible after adding the water. This will help keep it flaky and tender.

To make into a pie shell, roll out the dough on a lightly floured surface, forming a circle about 12 inches in diameter. Carefully transfer the dough to a 9-inch pie pan. Trim away any excess dough and crimp the edges.

To bake unfilled, preheat the oven to 450° F. Prick the pie shell all over with a fork and fill the bottom of the shell with dry beans. Bake in the preheated oven for about 8 minutes. Remove the beans and cook for an additional 2 to 4 minutes, or until the pie shell is evenly browned. Cool before filling.

YIELD: 9-INCH SINGLE CRUST PIE SHELL

147

Chin-Chin: Coffee & Exotic Drinks

Calypso Coffee

Island Coffee

Rum & Coconut Water

Grapefruit Juice & Rum

Bloody Mary à la Jerk

Frozen Daiquiri

Frozen Mango-Peach Daiquiri

Frozen Lime Daiquiri

Refreshing Rum Drink

Rum Punch

Planter's Punch

Mango-Papaya Punch

Tropical Fruit Punch

Marion's Fruit Pick-me-up

Pineapple Frappé

Aunt Becky's Jamaican Ginger Beer

Sorrel Drink

Tamarind-Ade

Simple Syrup

Jamaica, as everyone knows, is world famous for its Blue Mountain coffee. The soil in the higher altitudes of the Blue Mountains produces coffee that many people consider to be the best anywhere. There are many delicious ways to enjoy Jamaican coffee, including my favorite, Calypso Coffee, which is found in this chapter.

Because of our British heritage, Jamaicans are also big tea drinkers. For a spot o' tea we all take a break around four in the afternoon. Although the climate is hot, we learned from that other great English colony, India, to wear loose, lightweight clothing and to eat spicy foods and drink hot beverages to make us sweat. The evaporating perspiration makes us feel cooler.

In our houses there is always tea—real tea, not the "sissy" tea bags, or even the little tea balls, but real loose tea that is strained through beautiful silver strainers in the fancier homes, or through plain metal strainers in the simpler houses. Herbal teas are very popular, especially because you can just step outside your front door and pick a handful of herbs from your garden. Our regular tea is usually imported from India by way of Great Britain.

Of course, the popularity of tea is good news for our foremost local tea leaf reader, Mrs. DelGado. You will still see a long line of cars at her doorstep every afternoon. Her visitors are mostly politicians who think her advice is critical for their political survival, or ladies who are curious about the nocturnal activities of their husbands!

When I go to visit my friend Eli, she always has a beautiful tray waiting, set with a pot of tea, toast with guava jelly, banana bread, scones, coconut biscuits, or a light sandwich. In my mother's day, we had wonderful tea parties, with blue willow dishes from China. Sometimes we would read the tea leaves.

In general, the ladies of Jamaica, as the women like to be

called, are not big drinkers of alcohol. The men, however, seem to make up for us. You will see men sitting around the jerk shacks playing our national game, dominoes, drinking "whites" after "whites." A "whites," always referred to in the plural, is a stiff mix of high-proof rum and water. Truly a potent drink.

Then we have the ever-famous rum punch served at all parties and gatherings. The rule of thumb is to mix 1 portion of sour, 2 portions of sweet, 3 portions of strong, 4 portions of weak. With this little rhyme, you can mix up many variations, depending on what you have on hand. A typical punch might contain lime juice (sour), grenadine syrup (sweet), rum (strong), and another fruit juice, such as orange juice (weak). I like a touch of freshly grated nutmeg as a little garnish.

When you go to Jamaica, you will see that coconuts provide one of the main drinks of the island. The coconuts are picked much younger than those that you see in this country. Indeed, the coconuts are so young that they still have their husks on. Coconut meat of mature coconuts is not like the meat of the young coconuts sold in Jamaica. Instead there is a jelly-like substance and then a delicious pure sweet water inside. Folklore says this coconut water is the best cure for your kidney problems.

Along the roadside you will see mounds of fresh coconuts being prepared by the coconut man with his machete. When I was a child, the coconut man would pass by the house on his dray pulled by donkeys and filled with coconuts. He would shout, "Coconut, coconut!" We would shout back, "Coconut man, coconut man!" and he would know to stop. We would rush out to the gate and try to climb on the dray to select our coconut. Then the coconut man would chop a little hole in the jelly and give it to the buyer, who held this enormous coconut to his or her mouth and drank and drank. Ah . . . what a thirst quencher!

When we were finished, we'd hand the coconut back to the coconut man, who deftly chopped out a thin slice of the shell with his machete, and then quickly chopped open the nut. We'd scrape the inside of the nut with the coconut spoon supplied by the coconut man, and then devour all the jelly. This is the healthiest food that there is. At home we always had a jug of coconut water and coconut jelly in the refrigerator.

We also had the custom, leftover from colonial times, of having drinks in the late afternoon. My mother was fond of rum and ginger and she would lift her glass and say "Chin-Chin" to anyone who was with her.

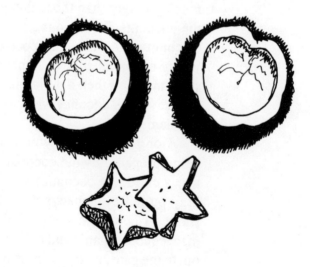

Calypso Coffee

2 cups hot Jamaican Blue
    Mountain coffee
1 tablespoon sugar
1 ounce Jamaican dark
    rum
3 ounces Tia Maria
Whipped cream to taste
Zest of 1 lime, cut in thin
    strips

Calypso Coffee is delicious only if served very hot, so I reheat my coffee in a saucepan. This is a drink that is sure to enhance your holiday season!

Heat the coffee in a saucepan just to simmering. Add the sugar, rum, and Tia Maria. Pour into large mugs or footed coffee glasses. Garnish with whipped cream and lime zest. Serve at once.

YIELD: 4 SERVINGS

Island Coffee

2 oranges
4 sugar cubes
⅔ cup whipping cream
⅔ cup confectioners' sugar
2 tablespoons butter, melted
¼ cup white sugar
½ cup brandy
5 tablespoons Grand Marnier or other orange liqueur
4 cups hot black coffee

This delicious coffee will make you think of the most elegant restaurants on the islands. It does take a few minutes to make the garnishes from the oranges, but the final effect is well worth the effort.

Rub both oranges with the sugar cubes to get some of the oil from the orange skin onto the sugar. Remove thin strips of zest from one orange and reserve for garnish; then squeeze the juice from it. Cut the other orange into very thin slices.

Whip the cream with the confectioners' sugar and set aside for the garnish.

Mix the melted butter and granulated sugar in a saucepan, and then add the sugar cubes and orange juice. Heat over low heat. When all the sugar has dissolved, pour in the brandy and Grand Marnier. Ignite and let burn for 30 seconds.

Pour the hot coffee into your prettiest mugs or footed coffee cups and then add the orange mixture to taste, as well as a strip of orange zest. Garnish with the whipped cream mixture and slices of orange.

YIELD: 6 TO 8 SERVINGS

Rum & Coconut Water

1 young coconut
2 ounces white rum
1 dash bitters (optional)

This is the Jamaican man's drink. After Hurricane Gilbert in 1988, when there were few coconuts left on the north coast of the island, my husband had a very difficult time trying to get his favorite cure-all.

Cut off the tip of the coconut and drain out the water. You should get enough to fill a 6- to 8-ounce glass. Mix in the rum and bitters and prepare to enjoy.

YIELD: 1 SERVING

Grapefruit Juice & Rum

4 cups grapefruit juice
4 ounces very light rum
4 maraschino cherries

Pour 1 cup of grapefruit juice and 1 ounce of rum in each of 4 tall glasses. Add lots of ice and a cherry. Very refreshing.

YIELD: 4 SERVINGS

Bloody Mary à la Jerk

1 quart tomato juice
½ cup freshly squeezed
   lime or lemon juice
1 tablespoon Dry Jerk
   Seasoning (page 16)
1 cup light or dark rum
Generous dashes of hot
   pepper sauce to taste
Celery sticks and lime
   wedges for garnish

Combine the tomato juice, lime juice, and Dry Jerk Seasoning. Heat and bring to a boil. Allow to cool. Add the rum and pepper sauce. Serve chilled in a pitcher garnished with celery sticks and lime wedges.

YIELD: 6 TO 8 SERVINGS

Frozen Daiquiri

3 cups crushed ice
6 ounces light rum
¼ cup Triple Sec
¼ cup Simple Syrup
    (page 171) or 2
    tablespoons white sugar
1 ounce lime juice
Orange slices and
    maraschino cherries for
    garnish

A daiquiri, to my mind, is one of the most romantic of drinks. This semi-frozen slush usually is served in an open champagne glass, garnished with a cherry, a sprig of mint, and pieces of mango or some other fruit. As most Americans know, daiquiris are made from fresh fruits with rum and ice. The pastel colors of the drink vary, depending on the fruit or juice that flavors it.

In a blender, combine the crushed ice with the rum, Triple Sec, simple syrup, and lime juice. Blend for about 40 seconds, or until slushy. Pour into champagne glasses and serve with small drink straws. Garnish each drink with orange slices and a cherry.

YIELD: 4 SERVINGS

Frozen Mango-Peach Daiquiri

Ice
1 cup peeled and sliced mango
1 cup canned sliced peaches
½ cup light rum
¼ cup sugar
Juice of 1 lime or lemon

Fill a blender ¾ full with ice, then add the other ingredients. Blend until slushy. Pour into champagne glasses to serve. This version will be a pale golden color.

YIELD: 2 TO 4 SERVINGS

Frozen Lime Daiquiri

Ice
1 (6-ounce) can frozen
  limeade
9 ounces light rum
2 ounces sweetened
  condensed milk
2 drops green food
  coloring
Lime slices for garnish

Fill a blender ¾ full with ice. Add the limeade, rum, milk, and food coloring. Blend until smooth. Pour into champagne glasses and garnish with slices of lime.

YIELD: 4 SERVINGS

Refreshing Rum Drink

3 ounces white rum
2 tablespoons lime juice
1 tablespoon Simple Syrup
  (page 171)
Club soda, well chilled
Lime wedges for garnish

Wonderful for extremely hot temperatures—say, after a long day on a pineapple plantation tour.

Combine the rum, lime juice, and sugar syrup in an ice-filled shaker. Shake well and then strain into 2 tall glasses filled with ice. Fill the rest of the way with the club soda and garnish with the lime wedges.

YIELD: 2 SERVINGS

Rum Punch

1 cup lime or lemon juice
   (Sour)
2 cups grenadine syrup
   (Sweet)
2 cups Jamaican white
   rum (Strong)
1 cup light rum (Strong)
2 cups pineapple juice
   (Weak)
2 cups orange juice
   (Weak)
½ teaspoon freshly grated
   nutmeg

Remember the formula: 1 portion of sour, 2 portions of sweet, 3 portions of strong, 4 portions of weak.

Mix together all the ingredients at least 1 hour before serving. Chill well. This punch looks beautiful served in a punch bowl with a pretty ice ring layered with orange slices and cherry halves.

YIELD: 18 TO 20 SERVINGS

Planter's Punch

8 ounces rum
  (light or dark)
¼ cup lime juice
¼ cup grenadine syrup
½ cup sugar
¼ cup orange juice
¼ cup pineapple juice
Pineapple spears or
  orange slices
  (optional garnish)

Mix together the rum, lime juice, grenadine, sugar, orange juice, and pineapple juice. Chill well. Serve in tall frosted glasses over cracked ice. Garnish with the pineapple spears if desired.

YIELD: 4 SERVINGS

Mango-Papaya Punch

1 small papaya
1 (19-ounce) can mango
  nectar
1 cup sugar
3 cups water
Juice of 2 limes
1 liter club soda
3 ounces light rum
  (optional)

Peel the papaya and remove its seeds. Combine the papaya, mango nectar, sugar, water, and lime juice in a blender. Process for approximately 30 seconds, or until well blended. Chill for at least 1 hour. Mix in the club soda and rum just before serving. Serve in your most attractive punch cups. If possible, decorate the punch bowl with hibiscus blossoms.

YIELD: 8 TO 10 SERVINGS

Tropical Fruit Punch

2 cups orange juice
2 cups pineapple juice
1 cup guava juice
12 ounces club soda
Grated fresh nutmeg
  to taste

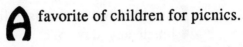 favorite of children for picnics.

Mix all ingredients, chill, and enjoy.

YIELD: 6 SERVINGS

Marion's Fruit Pick-me-up

2 ripe bananas
½ very, very ripe papaya
   (approximately
   2 cups pulp)
2 very ripe mangoes
   (approximately
   2 cups pulp)
Juice of 2 limes
1 (14-ounce) can
   sweetened condensed
   milk
½ cup water
3 cups pineapple juice
1 (46-ounce) can tropical
   fruit punch
Freshly grated nutmeg, for
   garnish

I would rather have this delicious concoction than a regular lunch any day. We always bought fresh fruit from the country on a Saturday morning. On the following Friday, if all the fresh fruits had not been eaten, they were put into the blender and made into a rich fruit drink for everyone.

Mix all the ingredients in a blender and process until smooth. Serve with lots of ice and a grating of fresh nutmeg on top. Delicious and very nutritious.

YIELD: 12 SERVINGS

Pineapple Frappé

1 pineapple, peeled and
  cored
1 cup sugar
3 tablespoons fresh cream
  or sweetened condensed
  milk
Crushed ice
Fresh mint leaves or
  freshly grated nutmeg
  (optional) for garnish

Cut the pineapple into chunks and combine in a blender with the sugar and cream. Fill the container approximately ¾ full with the ice. Blend until smooth and of icy consistency. Garnish with mint and serve in your prettiest open champagne glasses.

YIELD: 6 SERVINGS

Aunt Becky's Jamaican Ginger Beer

1 hand (4 to 6 inches) fresh
  ginger root, peeled and
  grated
1 tablespoon active dry
  (baker's) yeast
4 quarts water
4 cups sugar
½ cup dark rum (optional)

Ginger from Jamaica is renowned for the strength of the oil it contains. The combination of soil type and location has caused Jamaica to produce some of the finest spices and tropical fruits in the world. There are none like them anywhere else. Aunt Becky was a wonderful family friend who always supplied us with ginger beer from a recipe handed down through her family for many generations. Her family always used a version made with yeast, which I prefer, although several recipes do not use the yeast for fermentation. She also used a wonderful container called a *yabba* in which to ferment her ginger beer. *Yabbas* are large natural clay containers glazed only on the inside. Brought to Jamaica from Africa, they are the traditional holders of everything from ginger beer to Christmas pudding and sorrel drink. While you probably have no *yabbas* at home, you can still enjoy making ginger beer in a large stainless steel pot, glass bowl, or ceramic jug.

Combine the ginger, yeast, water, and sugar in a large crock or pot. Set outside for a day. A temperature of 80° F. is perfect for fermentation. Add rum if you wish, or wait and add it to each glass as you serve, for those who like a stronger drink. Strain, bottle, and refrigerate. The ginger beer will keep for up to 1 week.

YIELD: 12 SERVINGS

Sorrel Drink

2 ounces dried sorrel
  (available wherever
  Caribbean foods are
  sold)
1 finger (about 1 inch
  long) fresh ginger root,
  peeled and mashed
2 quarts boiling water
Approximately 3 cups
  sugar (depending on
  how sweet you want it)
½ cup rum (optional)

We always planted our sorrel in time to be ready at Christmas, although legend has it that Christmas is when the sorrel will be ready, regardless of when you plant! At any rate, the first thing you will hear when you visit any house at Christmas is, "Have a glass of sorrel. Ours is the best you will find this year!"

Combine the sorrel and ginger in a large bowl, or a *yabba* if you have one. Pour the boiling water over all and let it steep for at least a day. Strain through a sieve and then add the sugar. Add the rum if desired. Chill well. Serve over ice.

YIELD: 6 TO 8 SERVINGS

Tamarind-Ade

15 to 20 tamarind pods
1 cup sugar
6 cups warm water
Cold water to taste
Sugar to taste (you will
    need a great deal)

The tamarind is a large tree with long brown pod-type fruits originally found in India, but grown in Jamaica since the 1700s. It is well known as a thirst quencher. At home, we would keep a big pitcher of Tamarind-ade in the refrigerator to offer to guests and visitors. It is also frequently served with ginger ale for a dressier event.

You can find tamarind pods (or tamarind concentrate) in most Hispanic and Caribbean food stores.

Remove the long thin outer shell of the tamarind pods. Combine the pods and the 1 cup sugar in the warm water and let soak for 30 to 40 minutes. Strain and push the pulp through the strainer with a spoon or pestle. Discard the seeds and membranes that are left in the sieve. You are now left with the pulp of the tamarind, which is both very, very tart and very, very strong. It must be diluted or it will cut out your gullet! Of course, it is this very tartness that provides the well-known thirst-quenching qualities of the tamarind. Dilute with cold water and add sugar to taste. Serve chilled.

YIELD: 6 TO 8 SERVINGS

Simple Syrup

1 cup water
1 cup sugar

In Jamaica, we use grenadine syrup or a simple syrup to sweeten our drinks. Grenadine syrup is available commercially in the United States as well as in Jamaica and gives a wonderful pink color to any concoction. In the bars of the hotels, we use a simple syrup, which keeps for quite a few days. It is easier to dissolve in cold drinks than sugar.

Bring the water to boil in a small saucepan and stir in the sugar. Simmer for a few minutes until the sugar has dissolved. Cool.

YIELD: APPROXIMATELY 1 CUP

Sources of Caribbean Foods and Information

Many of recipes in this book can be made with commercial jerk seasoning mixes, rubs, and marinades. My own brand of jerk products, Helen's Tropical-Exotics, can be purchased in stores locally, or directly from my company. Please call (404) 292-7278 for more information or to place an order.

In general, Caribbean foods are not uncommon in the United States. In addition to countless bodegas, fresh produce stands, and specialty foods stores that stock Caribbean foods, many chain supermarkets stock Caribbean foods. Look for Goya-brand foods for high-quality canned and packaged Caribbean food products.

The following list includes businesses that sell fresh and packaged Caribbean foods in some areas of the United States and Canada. If no business is listed for your city, a phone call to the nearest listed business may provide you with information on how to find foods closer to home. Jampro (Jamaican Commerce Promotion and Information) is another source of information. Contact Deryk Cox, Senior Trade Commisioner, Jampro, 866 2nd Ave., 6th Floor, New York, NY 10017, (212) 371-4800. Another source of information is the Jamaica Tourist Board, 866 Second Avenue, 10th Floor, New York, NY 10017, (212) 688-7650; in Jamaica call (809) 929-9200.

California

Frieda's Finest Produce Specialties
P.O. Box 58488
Los Angeles, CA 90058
(213) 627-2981 (CA)
(800) 421-2981 (outside CA)
Exotic fruits and vegetables. Available by
mail order and for retail distribution.

G.B. Ratto International Grocers
821 Washington St.
Oakland, CA 94607
(800) 228-3515 (CA)
(800) 325-3483 (except CA)

Gourmet Specialties
228 Shaw Rd.
San Francisco, CA 94080
(415) 583-5900
A distributor of Helen's Tropical-Exotics
products.

Jones & Bones
621 Capitola Ave.
Capitola, CA 95010
(408) 462-0521
Carry a selection of Caribbean condiments,
sauces, and spices. Available by mail order.

Stone Bakery and Grocery Co.
6700 S. Crenshaw Blvd.
Los Angeles, CA 90043
(213) 753-3847

Florida

Blue Mountain Imports, Inc.
7022 N.W. 50th St.
Miami, FL 33166
(305) 594-9244
Caribbean sauces and marmalades. Available for retail stores.

De Jamaican Shop
4200 N.W. 12th St.
Lauderhill, FL 33313
(305) 581-3990
Grocery and take-out delicatessen.

Goya
1900 N.W. 92nd Ave.
Miami, FL 33172
(305) 592-3150

Jamaica Groceries & Spices
9628 S.W. 160th St.
Colonial Shopping Centre
Miami, FL 33157
(305) 252-1197

J. R. Brooks and Son, Inc.
P.O. Drawer 9
18400 SW 256th St.
Homestead, FL 33090-0009
(800) 423-4808 (FL)
(800) 327-4833 (outside FL)
(800) 338-1022 (Canada)
Tropical fruits.

Kingston-Miami Trading Co.
280 N.E. 2nd St.
Miami, FL 33132
(305) 372-9547
or
1500 N.W. 22nd St.
Miami, FL 33142
(305) 324-0231

Krevatas Import-Export
P.O. Box 562019
Miami, FL 33156
(305) 253-8108

La Preferida, Inc. (Florida)
9108 N.W. 105th Way
Medley, FL 33178
(305) 883-8444
Contact: Carlos Bordon

McDonald Import Co., Inc.
300 N. Chrome Ave.
Florida City, FL 33034
or
P.O. Box 970134
Miami, FL 33197
(305) 246-1816

Temptations — Caribbean Harvest
P.O. Box 170105
Miami, FL 33017
Contact: Jackie Shepard

West Indian American Grocery
19571 N.W. 2nd Ave.
Miami, FL 33169
(305) 651-8455

West Indian Food Specialties
6035 Miramar Parkway
Miramar, FL 33023
(305) 962-6418

Georgia

Dekalb World Farmers Market
3000 E. Ponce de Leon
Decatur, GA 30034
(404) 377-6401
A wonderful source of foods from around
the world.

Dewars Fine Foods
1937 Peachtree Road
Atlanta, GA 30309
(404) 351-3663

Harry's Farmers Market
1180 Upper Hembree Rd.
Alpharetta, GA
(404) 664-6300

Helen's Tropical-Exotics
3519 Church St.
Clarkston, GA 30021
GA: (404) 292-7278
Wholesalers and retailers: (800) 544-JERK
Commercially prepared jerk seasonings,
marinades, dipping sauces, Scotch bonnet
pepper sauce, and tropical fruit sauces.

Illinois

Goya
2701 West Armitage Ave.
Chicago, IL 60647

La Preferida, Inc. (Chicago)
3400 W. 35th St.
Chicago, IL 60632
(312) 254-7200
Contact: William L. Steinberth,
 or Robert Gouwens

New Jersey

Goya Foods
100 Seaview Drive
Secaucus, NJ 07094
(201) 348-4900

LOI Industries, Inc.
205 Jackson St.

Englewood, NJ 07631
(201) 567-0800
Contact: Allen Baboian
Wholesale importer of Caribbean food
products

New York

Brooklyn Terminal Market
Liberty Ave.
Brooklyn, NY 11207

Casa Hispania International Food Market
PO Box 587
73 Poningo St.
Port Chester, NY 10578
(914) 939-9333

Dean & Deluca
560 Broadway, Suite 304
New York, NY 10012
(800) 221-7714 (except NY)
(800) 431-1691 (NY)
Call or write for a free catalog; they sell a
variety of imported and domestic specialty
foods.

Global Tropical Company
91-93 Brooklyn Terminal Market
Brooklyn, NY 11236
(718) 763-4603
Wholesale importer of Jamaican and
Caribbean food.

Island Cooking Kitchens
1245 Park Ave.
New York, NY 10028
(212) 860-8810
Jerk marinades under the Tradewinds label.
Contact: Dunstan Harris
Author of *Island Cooking*, The Crossing Press.

J'ai Besoin, Ltd.
11 Meriden Place
West Hills, NY 11747
(516) 424-5353
Contact: Conni Gothelf-Kalman
A distributor of Helen's Tropical-Exotics products.

Jamaica Originals, Ltd.
P.O. Box 1242
Murray Hill Station
New York, NY 10156

La Marqueta
Park Ave. at 116th St.
New York, NY 10029
(212) 996-1930

Port Royal Foods, Inc.
P.O. Box 881
Hicksville, NY 11802
Contact: Irving Zwecker

Seyoum International
361 Broadway Suite 510
New York, NY 10013
Research and marketing of food products from the Caribbean for export and manufacturing.

Tropica Island Traders
170 Fifth Ave. and Twenty Second St.
New York, NY 10010
(212) 627-0808
Specializing in products from the Caribbean.

Texas

La Preferida, Inc. (Texas)
4000 Telephone Rd.
Houston, TX 77087
(713) 643-7128
Contact: Edgar Martinez

Canada

Central West Indies Grocery
252 Queen Street East
Eastown Plaza
Brampton, Ont.
(416) 453-8084

Elma's Spice Corner
2560 Shepard Ave. S.
King & Shepard Plaza #4
Mississauga, Ont. A58 2H6
(416) 277-0557

Harvey W.I. Food Store
2545 Hurontario St.
Mississauga, Ont.
(416) 272-4950

Solas Market
341 Glendower Circuit
Agincourt
Toronto, Ont.
(416) 291-6567

Toronto Caribbean Corner
57 Kensington Ave.
Toronto, Ont.
(416) 593-0008

Tropical Harvest Food Market
57 Kensington Ave.
Toronto, Ont.
(416) 593-9279

West Indian Fine Foods
Terrace Brae Plaza
Markham & Lawrence
Scarborough, Ont.
(416) 431-9353

Index

If you would like to learn more about the cuisine of the Caribbean, we suggest *Island Cooking, Recipes from the Caribbean* by Dunstan A. Harris; The Crossing Press, 1988.

The Crossing Press publishes
a full selection of cookbooks.
To receive our current catalog,
please call
TOLL FREE 800/777-1048.